Praise for *The Sabbath of the Land*

"In this brilliant translation of Rav Kook's work and in his accompanying essays, Yedidya Sinclair succeeds in clarifying the paradoxes of shemitta. His historical, biographical, and conceptual introduction is cogent and elegant; it is supplemented by a thoughtful analysis of broader environmental and social justice values now being seriously discussed in Israel. A highly valuable and enlightening volume."

– Dr. Avivah Gottlieb Zornberg
Author of *The Murmuring Deep: Reflections on the Biblical Unconscious*

"The colossal figure of Rav Kook challenges all his readers – be they students, scholars, teachers, activists, and above all, anyone trying to live by eternal truths in rapidly changing times – and his translators too. Those who can scale those heights offer immense rewards, and Yedidya Sinclair, the kind of scholar-pioneer Rav Kook hoped to see, is one of them. He renders Rav Kook into beautiful, crystalline English while retaining the Hebrew original's poetic force, provides essential historical, theological and halakhic context that illuminates the work without submerging it, and powerfully conveys the contemporary stakes of this effort – for Judaism, Zionism, social justice, ecology and much more – which, more than a century after Rav Kook wrote – grow more urgent by the day. If you have time for just one book on the upcoming Shemitta year, this is it."

– Dr. Yehudah Mirsky
Professor of Near Eastern and Judaic Studies, Brandeis University
Author of *Rav Kook: Mystic in a Time of Revolution* and *Towards the Mystical Experience of Modernity*

"I am pleased to express the great significance of the Maggid-Hazon edition of Rav Kook's *Shabbat HaAretz,* skillfully translated and meaningfully introduced by Rabbi Julian Sinclair. This masterpiece demonstrates how the first Chief Rabbi of modern Eretz Israel was able to maintain the biblical ideals of the Sabbatical and Jubilee years despite our rapidly changing economy; moreover, it also mediates in a most timely manner the debate between capitalism and socialism as well as emphasizing on the Sabbatical Year our communal responsibility to the individual debtor as well as to the land itself (ecology, to "develop and protect" our natural resources, Gen. 2:15). Rav Kook's arguments as developed by the commentary of Julian Sinclair greatly enhance our understanding of the sanctity of our Land, and the eternal relevance of our Sacred Scripture as we include the interpretations of the Sages of every generation (*Torah shebe'al peh*)."

– Rabbi Shlomo Riskin
Founding Rabbi of Efrat
Rosh Yeshiva, Ohr Torah Stone

"There are few concepts as beautiful (and as radical) as the Jewish idea of a sabbath for the land every seven years. [As is seen] in this utterly fascinating translation, Rav Kook offers a gorgeous and profound hymn from across the decades to the concept, and the able translator provides historical context as well as powerful hope that this great rest and rejuvenation can have practical as well as spiritual meaning in the modern age."

– Bill McKibben
Author of *Deep Economy: The Wealth of Communities and the Durable Future*

"Rarely can a one-hundred-year-old pamphlet reach across history and shake a reader's heart and inspire an activist's hands. *Shabbat HaAretz,* which was revolutionary in the Land of Israel in its time and is revolutionary for American Jews today, does just that. Hazon and Sinclair have done us an enormous service by bringing Rav Kook's Introduction to *Shabbat HaAretz* into the heart of 21st-century living."

– Rabbi Mishael Zion
Coauthor of *A Night to Remember: The Haggadah of Contemporary Voices*

"If Britain and America are two countries divided by a common language, then Israel is a country, and the Jewish people a people, divided by a common religion. Rav Kook is still, a century on, sorely missed as a religious leader who deeply believed in finding ways for observant and non-observant Jews to build the same country together. Every seven years we see how his work, *Shabbat HaAretz,* is not only still relevant, but even more necessary than ever."

– Saul Singer
Coauthor, *Start-Up Nation: The Story of Israel's Economic Miracle*

"Since the time when Rav Kook penned *Shabbat HaAretz,* humanity's relentless exploitation of the earth has accelerated to the point where much of the destruction is irreversible. Rabbi Julian Sinclair's translation and commentary of Rav Kook elevates our consciousness to a new level so that indeed we come to realize that understanding the spiritual greatness of shemitta is a prerequisite for taking the practical steps that can reverse climate change, feed the hungry, and even cloth the naked. What I learned from this holy book is that the seeds of humanity's redemption live within the radical notion of shemitta."

– Yosef Abramowitz
Cofounder and CEO, Energiya Global

"We are in the debt of Rabbi Julian Sinclair, among the greatest expositors of Rav Kook's thought and writing in English, for providing us with this edition of *Shabbat HaAretz* in which we encounter a vision for revived Jewish existence and society in the Land of Israel."

– Rabbi Jeffrey Saks
Editor, *Tradition: A Journal of Orthodox Jewish Thought*

The Sabbath of the Land

Selections from Rav Kook's *Shabbat HaAretz* and Contemporary Reflections on Renewing Shemitta

hazon
THE JEWISH LAB FOR SUSTAINABILITY

מגיד
MAGGID

Rabbi Abraham Isaac Kook

The Sabbath **of the Land**

Selections from Rav Kook's
Shabbat HaAretz
and Contemporary Reflections on Renewing Shemitta

TRANSLATION AND COMMENTARY BY
Yedidya J. Sinclair

Hazon
Maggid Books

The Sabbath of the Land
Selections from Rav Kook's Shabbat HaAretz
and Contemporary Reflections on Renewing Shemitta

First Edition, 2021

Maggid Books
An imprint of Koren Publishers Jerusalem Ltd.

POB 8531, New Milford, CT 06776-8531, USA
& POB 4044, Jerusalem 9104001, Israel
www.maggidbooks.com

English translation of *Shabbat HaAretz* Halakhot first published
in *Jewish Legal Theories*, Brandeis University Press, 2018.

The publication of this book was made possible
through the generous support of *The Jewish Book Trust.*

ISBN 978-1-59264-593-0, *hardcover*

Printed and bound in the United States

Contents

Foreword

Why Shemitta Is Not Just for Farmers

Nigel Savage*

Seven years have gone by since our first edition, which was published on the eve of the shemitta year of 5775, in 2014–15. That year saw growing interest in, and awareness of, the profundity and relevance of shemitta as a concept. And yet we have barely scratched the surface of what is possible and necessary in relation to shemitta.

I want to offer two reasons why I think shemitta has been overlooked.

First, shemitta seems to be about *farming*. Indeed, in Israel, every seven years, there is an argument about which fruit and vegetables you can eat. This was the impetus for the publication of *Shabbat HaAretz*

* Nigel Savage founded Hazon in 2000. Previously he was a professional fund manager in London, where he worked for NM Rothschild and was co-head of UK Equities at Lovett. He has an MA in History from Georgetown, and has studied at Pardes, Yakar, and the Hebrew University. He has twice been named to the Forward 50, and in 2015, in recognition of his work, he was awarded an honorary doctorate by the Jewish Theological Seminary. He is thought to be the first English Jew to have cycled across South Dakota on a recumbent bike.

in 1909, in the first place. But apart from the question of what you can eat in Israel – and perhaps because of that, also – it is easy to read the primary texts of shemitta as if they were "beautiful" or "inspiring," but otherwise entirely removed from normal life for most people today, since most of us are not farmers.

To my mind this is a mistake, or at the very least, a misconception. We forget that the land of Israel twenty centuries ago was an agrarian society. The teachings of shemitta were thus not only about *farming*, narrowly construed, in our terms; they were about *life*. "Shemitta" was addressing issues today encompassed by culture, economics, education, ecology and, perhaps overarchingly, political philosophy: how people self-organize equitably and peaceably.

So I invite you to see this book as the beginning of redressing this misconception, in how *you* think about shemitta, and in how you talk about it with others. Shemitta is or should be critical to what it means to be Jewish today, and to a range of major challenges confronting Israeli and Diaspora Jews.

For Israeli Jews: How does the concept of shemitta challenge this sovereign state to craft a Jewish commonwealth which embodies the great aspirations and high standards of Jewish tradition? Helping those in need. Caring for the land itself. Being concerned for the welfare of animals. Seeking to ensure availability of credit, while finding ways to release people crippled by too much debt. Breaking down barriers, literal and metaphorical. Seeing every member of society as playing their own unique role in society.

For Diaspora Jews, a distinct but related challenge. The larger issues mentioned above are in the headlines every day. Shemitta thus invites us to ask if the Jewish community has anything distinct to add to the public conversation. The arguments between "progressives," "liberals," "conservatives," and "populists" have grown more unpleasant these last seven years – unpleasant, and also in some ways stale. There is a temptation simply to plug in to these political tribes, gluing Jewish tradition somewhat awkwardly into contemporary political frames. This does a disservice to the richness, complexity, utopianism, and practicality of the tradition. As you read this book you might ask yourself, *If I were to try to allow these teachings to guide me as a citizen of*

Israel, or the United States, or anywhere else, how might they inflect what I say, or do, or advocate for?

Rabbi Jonathan Sacks, of blessed memory, taught that while it is unwise to align Jewish tradition with specific political parties and movements, it is vital to allow the uniqueness and richness of the tradition to inform the wider contemporary political and cultural conversation. In that sense, this book, which aims to introduce Rav Kook's teachings to the wider world, also takes inspiration from the teachings of Rabbi Sacks.

There is a second reason that shemitta has been overlooked, and a second distinct way that I hope we can continue to bring the wisdom of shemitta to more people, more deeply. This second aspect is, in a sense, distinct from the content of shemitta; it begins simply by thinking about shemitta as *a seven-year frame in time.*

It is striking that we do indeed overlook it in this sense. The Jewish world runs on Jewish time, and this is true across all distinctions of place and denomination. In any Jewish institution Tuesday is different from Shabbat; Pesaḥ is different from Rosh HaShana; Purim is different from Ḥanukka; and so on. The only exception – the *only* exception – is shemitta.

The reason is twofold. First, in relation to shemitta, there's nothing we have to do, or not do. Certainly for a Diaspora Jew there are, in practice, no halakhot – no religious injunctions – that (unlike every other distinct Jewish date) prescribe or proscribe behavior. It is thus very easy to ignore or forget shemitta. For Israeli Jews it is only a half-step further. For an observant Israeli Jew there *are* practical questions raised by shemitta, preeminently the question that prompted Rav Kook to write *Shabbat HaAretz* in the first place: What fruit and vegetables can or should I eat during the shemitta year? But this question, real though it is, continues to obscure all the other ways that Israeli Jews could be thinking about shemitta – but in general are not.

And second, and linked to this, unlike every other date on the Jewish calendar, shemitta has no associated rituals. What would be our relationship to Shabbat without Shabbat candles, or Havdala? Or to Sukkot, without the *lulav* and *etrog* – and the sukka? Would we register the fourth or the seventh night of Ḥanukka if we didn't light Ḥanukka candles every night? Would it be Rosh HaShana without apples and honey, or the different Mizraḥi food traditions? What would Pesach be without Seder, or the Haggada, or *Ḥad Gadya*? And so on. Our tradition is beautiful and wise in the way that the marking of time interweaves three things: the actual time of Shabbat and the festivals, i.e., the distinctiveness of that particular unit of time; then the particular rituals that reinforce and signify the observance of these different times; and then – and this is arguably the most important of all – the wider lessons that we derive for our lives and for our behaviors, *from* Shabbat and the festivals. Rosh HaShana and Yom Kippur are on specific dates, and they have specific rituals; but their actual focus is *teshuva*, the question of how we return, repent, make amends. The interrelationship of time, ritual, and meaning is so obvious, so central to Jewish life, that we take it for granted – and thus miss the significance of the *absence* of ritual reinforcement and time delineation in the case of shemitta.

There are two things we must do in relation to these two challenges.

The first is simply choosing to mark shemitta as a frame in time, and encouraging our families, our friends, and our institutions to do likewise.

As the shemitta year approaches, it is a time to start to prepare for *shnat shemitta*. We should ask: *How will this year be different for me, for my family, for my institution?* How should we observe and respect it?

Then the shemitta year itself. A time to look back and a time to look forward. Where was I six years ago? What have I learned, what has changed? How do I live more lightly? How do I consume less? How do I strive to ameliorate inequality in my community – so that "the needy of your people may eat" (Ex. 23:11)? And – a deep visioning exercise – where will I, or we, be seven years from now? What is my vision for myself, my family, my community, looking out over that time horizon?

And the third period is, of course, the next full seven-year shemitta cycle in Jewish life. In the Torah, this new cycle is marked by *hakhel* (Deut. 31:10–12), a national convocation to renew the covenant with the Torah. I would argue that *hakhel* stands in relation to shemitta the way that Havdala does in relation to Shabbat – both an end and a beginning. (And it is significant that *hakhel* is a national and political event, involving the king, the priests, and *all* of the people, a point which the Torah goes out of its way to emphasize. In and of itself, *hakhel*, which marks the conclusion of the shemitta year, comes to remind us of some of the larger messages of shemitta.)

So we should take steps to mark shemitta time in Jewish life, just as we mark every other distinct period in Jewish life; and, as with Pesah (in relation to liberation from enslavement) or Rosh HaShana and Yom Kippur (in relation to *teshuva*), the whole shemitta year should be a time to engage with the themes of shemitta, and to ask how we could or should address them today.

And second – and going back to the absence of ritual – I think we should take steps to engender our own "rituals." Just a little while after writing the first preface to this book, seven years ago, I found myself wondering how I might remind myself of the forthcoming shemitta year. Somewhat randomly – but not entirely randomly – I decided that I would not buy any books or Scotch whisky during the shemitta year. The first of these ideas stressed me out so much that, for several months prior to Rosh HaShana, I went around my apartment, taking off the shelves either books that I hadn't yet read, or books that I had read but wanted to reread. I wrapped them in newspaper – unmarked – and stacked them up. Then if, during the shemitta year, the urge to buy a new book finally became too great to bear, I could simply take one of these, unwrap it, and delightedly say, *Gosh, I always wanted to read this!*

I made this commitment, as we say, *bli neder:* maybe I would stick to it and maybe I would not; we would see. And the same with not buying Scotch. I wasn't prohibiting myself from buying wine or beer, so this was hardly a huge hardship. But, in these two ways, I wanted to try to remind myself that it was the shemitta year – distinct from the other six years of the cycle.

And what happened was fascinating. First, I was indeed reminded, repeatedly, that the year was different. Every time I thought about buying a book (i.e., frequently) and every time I offered someone a Scotch (i.e., not infrequently) I was reminded that this was the shemitta year. And, more remarkably, I indeed didn't buy a single book, nor did I open a single one of the books I had wrapped. And because people brought gifts of Scotch (unasked, not knowing about my not buying Scotch), my liquor cabinet miraculously lasted the whole year. The lesson – in both cases – was that *I had enough.* Had, indeed, more than I needed.

Yet a couple of years ago, reflecting on this, I realized I was also missing one key aspect of shemitta's teaching. Shemitta is more than simply letting go or consuming less; it is also about *helping those who have less in the first place.* For this shemitta year I've decided again not to buy books or Scotch, and this time not to buy clothes also; but I've also decided to figure out what I spend on those things in a normal year, and give that instead directly to people in need.

And this is just one small step toward the deeper lessons of shemitta. As Rav Kook repeatedly stresses, the goals and the vision of shemitta are ultimately societal. It's about a lot more than whether we do or do not buy books or clothes or Scotch. But Jewish tradition teaches us, through daily practice, about the interweaving of ritual, personal behavior, and communal and societal vision. This is why it is important that in this edition we have begun to translate the halakhic parts of *Shabbat HaAretz.* High ideals and a great vision are important. But in Jewish life, high ideals make their presence felt in daily practice. Establishing actionable ways to mark the shemitta year will be significant if they help remind us of the larger lessons of shemitta and inspire us in our behaviors to touch people's lives for good.

This year, thinking about this, inspired by Rabbi Nina Beth Cardin, and with the support of Marc and Karyn Schiller and the partnership in Israel of the Shalom Hartman Institute, we have launched a series of Shemitta Prizes, precisely to encourage new ideas and new rituals – and interesting ideas are starting to sprout. Shoshana Gugenheim Kedem, for example, envisioned shemitta tableware, to grace our tables during the shemitta year and to remind us of the values of shemitta every time we eat. Rachel Jackson and Jackson Mercer are working on public crates, modeled on the pop-up libraries, and inspired directly by the provisions of shemitta, which could be situated outside public institutions, for people to deposit canned food, or fresh fruits and vegetables – and for others simply to help themselves to them. My friend Daniel Taub suggested quite simply that every Diaspora Jew commit to study Hebrew during the shemitta year – and every Israeli Jew commit to study Arabic.

The Institute for Jewish Spirituality is thinking about shemitta in relation to *middot,* the ongoing process of striving to improve one's behaviors. On a larger public scale, Shaul Goldstein, the long-time head of the Israel Nature and Parks Authority, has adopted the shemitta idea as a frame to develop closer connection and responsibility between Israel's inhabitants and the Land of Israel. INPA is developing a campaign to encourage a million people to commit to clean up the country during the shemitta year –both to make a practical difference, and to change public consciousness in relation to littering and harming the natural world.

So shemitta is coming to life in new and fresh ways. And yet we have indeed barely scratched it. This is why it is important to read Rav Kook – to think anew about how great is the ideal, how great the challenge, and how very far we are from bringing any serious version of it to fruition.

And as we think about shemitta, we now have the frame of Covid to offer further perspective. Covid helps us understand shemitta afresh, and shemitta in turn may be uniquely valuable in framing thoughtful post-Covid conversations. This is precisely what we mean by "The Torah is a commentary on the world, and the world is a commentary on the Torah."

The challenging and disruptive period that began in March 2020 was, like a shemitta year, marked by significant changes to "normal" life. Many of us experienced both sides of this – that which was hard, and that which was positive. There was enforced immobility: not being able to go to an office, a restaurant, a place of work. There was physical disruption, economic disruption. Loss of physical community; not being able to see people, or hug people. Yet, on the other hand, and amidst all the hardships, there were for many unexpected compensations. We "got back to basics." We saw fewer people and connected with those who were most important to us. Traveling less was good for the world. Many people have commented on the extent to which it was a year of clarification – thinking about choices, vision, the sort of lives we want to lead. Having a year to step back, live more lightly, think about big choices – this is also what shemitta is about. I hope that, in future decades, we will be able to learn some of these lessons from shemitta, without having first to endure a global pandemic.

Covid also threw into relief some of the challenges that shemitta seeks to address. Inequality increased. People with means were mostly okay. People who had less money, fewer health resources, and weaker school systems suffered far more. Post-Covid, many governments are trying to address these issues. We cannot try to map a biblical concept directly onto our complex postmodern world. But the questions raised by shemitta – and the deep humanity implied by its provisions – can and should help us face these challenges.

This applies, for instance, to *shemittat kesafim*, the prescription to annul debts in a shemitta year. Aggregate student debt in the United States has increased by nearly half a trillion dollars since the start of the last shemitta year. Is that healthy, or viable, or wise – and what, if at all, is to be done about it? And how should Western governments – including the Israeli government – redress financial hardships endured by the poorest in our societies, because of Covid? These are real questions, and there are no simple answers. My point is that we should allow the teachings of shemitta, and this seminal contribution of Rav Kook, to inform our values; and our values, in turn, to influence public policy. In summary: *Shemitta, at its core, is about envisioning a world of radical equality and freedom.* That is what should inspire and provoke us today.

I end with *hakarat hatov* – great gratitude. I'm so excited that this revised and enlarged edition of *Shabbat HaAretz* is being published. I am delighted that Maggid has chosen to publish this new edition, and I thank Matthew Miller, Reuven Ziegler, Ita Olesker, and their team for their confidence in this project.

The somewhat different foreword to the first edition is online at hazon.org/shabbathaaretz and I'm happy to point you there, not only for additional comments but also to acknowledge the many people who helped bring the first edition to fruition. In addition to them, and the people already mentioned, I want to thank Rabbi Sam Feinsmith, Michal Fox Smart, Hannah Knibb Henza, Jack Henza, Dr. Rani Jaeger, Shira Hecht Koller, Rabbi Aharon Ariel Lavi, Jakir Manela, Rabbi Dr. Adam Mintz, Irit Offer-Stark, Dayan Yehoshua Pfeffer, Dr. Renana Ravitzky Pilzer, Stefanie Raker, Rabbi Isaiah Rothstein, Bruce Spierer, Eliot Sacks, Rabbi Lewis Warshauer, and Sarah Zell Young for help, advice, inspiration, and ideas. I thank the growing number of organizations that have joined the Shemitta Project, our open-source platform to magnify the teachings of shemitta. I gratefully acknowledge the support of the Covenant Foundation and the Jim Joseph Foundation in enabling us to do this work.

I am again delighted to thank Jorian Polis Schutz for support both existential and practical. Jorian in his life and in his work continues to model the many different ways that we can and should try to bring these values and ideas to physical fruition.

And I am immensely grateful to the board, staff, and stakeholders of Hazon. Since 2007 they have supported and encouraged my fascination with this topic, and they have steadily advanced our work. This time around they have also enabled me to begin the shemitta year in Jerusalem…on sabbatical. Thank you!

Finally, I hope that anyone reading this book will realize not just how extraordinary Rav Kook was but also, in fact, what a remarkable teacher Rabbi Yedidya Sinclair is. One sees on every page of this book, in his introduction, in his translation, and in his notes, how deeply he combines immense Jewish learning with a thoughtful and serious engagement with the larger issues raised by shemitta. It is a tremendous achievement to produce such a superb, annotated translation of this rich, unique, and complex work, and I thank him very greatly, on behalf of all of us, for the great mitzva he has done.

May we be blessed to have the opportunities to rest, to renew, and to mark time in ways that create a healthier, more equitable, and more sustainable world for all.

Jerusalem
September 2021 / Elul 5781

Acknowledgments

This volume is an expanded version of a book that was published in September 2014 by Hazon. The debts I acknowledged then remain relevant to this new edition: It is a pleasure to thank Nigel Savage, director of Hazon, for his visionary initiative in suggesting and sponsoring this book; Jorian Polis Schutz for his enthusiastic and insightful support; Elisheva Urbas for her intelligent and meticulous editing, keeping me close to the rules wherever possible while helping avoid various barbarities; Janice Meyerson for her excellent copy editing; Jessica Sacks for generous and helpful comments; Richard Resnick, from whom I first heard of Rav Kook's extraordinary body of thought; Rabbi Hillel Rachmani for his profound lectures on this thought at Yeshivat Har Etzion; Professor Benjamin Ish-Shalom for his rigorous and inspiring introductory course on Rav Kook at Beit Morasha, and HaRav Shagar *z"l* for his remarkable *shiurim* on shemitta at the same institution; Professor Yehudah Mirsky for giving me prepublication sight of his superb biography of Rav Kook; Dr. Michael Kagan for years of encouragement and stimulating conversations about Judaism, economics, and the environment; Yosef Abramowitz and Weldon Turner for encouraging me to bring this book into conversation with our work at Energiya Global; and my wife, Yaffa Aranoff, for her close reading, broad knowledge of Jewish mystical writings, and immense support.

For the current edition, I add my gratitude to Professor Yonatan Brafman for his insightful comments on the translation of the halakhic sections from *Shabbat HaAretz*; to Brandeis University Press, and Professors Brafman and Leora Batnitzky, editors of the excellent "Jewish Legal Theories" anthology, in which some of the translated halakhic sections were first published in 2018; to Reuven Ziegler, Ita Olesker, Caryn Meltz, Aryeh Grossman, and everyone at Maggid Books for their enthusiastic support and meticulous editing; and to Rabbi Dov Berkovits, Rabbi David Ebner, Rabbi Dr. Benjamin Elton, David Jackson, Einat Kramer, Aharon Ariel Lavi, Rabbi Michael Melchior, Nigel Savage, and Rabbi Josh Weisberg for illuminating conversations and *ḥavrutot* about shemitta over the past seven years.

Yedidya J. Sinclair
Elul 2021/5781

Introduction

Rav Kook and the Meaning of Shemitta

Shabbat HaAretz, published by Rabbi Abraham Isaac Kook on the eve of the 1909–10 shemitta year, is undoubtedly the most important and influential book on shemitta to have appeared in the modern era. It is indispensable to understanding how shemitta is currently observed and not observed.[1] The context, arguments, and aftermath of *Shabbat HaAretz* remain formative forces upon the status of shemitta in the State of Israel. There is probably no more important text for understanding why shemitta is the way it is today.

But throughout *Shabbat HaAretz,* and particularly throughout its introduction, shines a vision of how shemitta could be much more than it is today. Rav Kook believed in the power of social and spiritual reawakening embodied in shemitta. He hoped that the leniency that enabled the land to be sold (*heter mekhira*) and, effectively, shemitta not to be observed, was a step on the journey toward the renewal of shemitta.

This introduction will outline some of the sources in Rav Kook's life and his work for his thinking on shemitta, summarize the outlines

1. For a comprehensive practical guide to the observance of shemitta, see Rabbi Yosef Zvi Rimon, *Shemita: From the Sources to the Practical Halacha* (Jerusalem: Yeshivat Har Etzion and Maggid Books, 2008).

of his halakhic argument in *Shabbat HaAretz*, and explore briefly the resources in Rav Kook's introduction to *Shabbat HaAretz* that point beyond the *heter mekhira* compromise to a fuller and richer observance of shemitta.

SHEMITTA

Three passages in the Torah discuss shemitta. Each passage reveals a different dimension of shemitta's values and practices. Let us briefly examine each section in turn.

> You shall not oppress a stranger, for you know the feelings of the stranger, having been yourselves strangers in the land of Egypt. Six years shall you sow your land and gather in your yield; but in the seventh year, you shall let it rest and lie fallow. Let the needy among your people eat of it; and what they leave, let the wild beasts eat. You shall do the same with your vineyards and your olive groves. Six days you shall do your work; but on the seventh day, you shall cease from labor, in order that your ox and ass may rest and that your bondsman and stranger may be refreshed. (Ex. 23:10–12)

The passage above focuses on the egalitarian aspect of shemitta. In the seventh year, agricultural work ceases, and the produce of the land becomes ownerless. The poor and needy enter into previously private fields, vineyards, and olive groves and eat the crops. Animals may come and eat what is left. Property rights in the land and its produce are erased; rich and poor, humans and beasts, all share what grows naturally in the shemitta year. The verses about shemitta are placed between the reminder not to oppress the stranger because we were once strangers in Egypt and a repetition of the command to keep Sabbath, which emphasizes the rights of your servants and animals to rest with you. This juxtaposition sites shemitta in the context of the Torah's concern for the poor, the marginalized, and the oppressed.

> When you enter into the land that I assign you, the land shall observe a Sabbath of the Lord. Six years you may sow your

> field, and six years you may prune your vineyard, and gather in the yield; but in the seventh year, the land shall have a Sabbath of complete rest, a Sabbath of the Lord: you shall not sow your field or prune your vineyard. You shall not reap the aftergrowth of your harvest or gather the grapes of your untrimmed vines. It shall be a year of complete rest for the land, but you may eat whatever the land will produce during its Sabbath – you, your male and female slaves, the hired and bound laborers who live with you, and your cattle and the beasts on your land may eat all its yield. (Lev. 25:2–7)

The Torah repeats the command to cease agricultural work in the seventh year, but the focus in the passage above is not on the poor but on the land. Just as people enjoy Sabbath one day out of seven, so, too, should the land have its Sabbath, one year out of seven. This is our duty of stewardship to the earth. We should not treat it as merely a resource to be endlessly exploited for our benefit; the land must also rest. During the land's Sabbath, we do not plant or cultivate it, and we eat only what grows by itself. Thus we show that we are not the land's ultimate masters. In this year, land is a place where humans, animals, and the earth itself meet on equal terms; there are no owners or exploiters but only fellow creatures.

> Every seventh year, you shall practice remission of debts. This shall be the nature of the remission: every creditor shall remit the due that he claims from his fellow; he shall not exact payment from his fellow or kinsman, for the remission proclaimed is of the Lord. You may exact payment from the foreigner, but you must remit whatever is due you from the kinsman.... If, however, there is a needy person among you, one of your kinsmen in any of your settlements in the land that the Lord your God is giving you, do not harden your heart or shut your hand against your needy kinsman. Rather, you must open your heart and lend him sufficient for whatever he needs. Beware, lest you harbor the base thought, the seventh year, the year of remission is approaching, so that you are mean to your needy kinsman and give him nothing.

> He will cry out to the Lord against you, and you will incur guilt. Give to him readily, and have no regrets when you do so, for in turn, the Lord your God will bless you in all your efforts and all your undertakings. (Deut. 15:1–3; 7–10)

The passage above adds a further dimension of shemitta: the remission of debts. Every seven years, debts are canceled. The crushing obligations of debtors that weigh them down and can permanently cripple their flourishing are lifted. (It may be meritorious for the debtor to repay the loan after the shemitta year, if he can, but he does not have to do so.) The Torah warns potential lenders against the suspicions that they may harbor of moral hazard in this situation. As the seventh year approaches, they should not withhold loans out of fear that the shemitta will wipe out the debt. Rather, they must know that lending to the needy is among the responsibilities of the propertied, in full knowledge that the sabbatical debt remission may intervene to cancel the loan.

JUBILEE

The Torah describes the Jubilee (*yovel*) as the culmination of seven cycles of shemitta observance:

> You shall count off seven weeks of years – seven times seven years – so that the period of seven weeks of years gives you a period of forty-nine years. Then you shall sound the horn loud; in the seventh month, on the tenth day of the month – the Day of Atonement – you shall have the horn sounded throughout your land, and you shall hallow the fiftieth year. You shall proclaim release throughout the land for all its inhabitants. It shall be a Jubilee for you: each of you shall return to his holding, and each of you shall return to his family. That fiftieth year shall be a Jubilee for you: you shall not sow, and neither shall you reap the aftergrowth nor harvest the untrimmed vines, for it is a Jubilee. It shall be holy to you: you may eat only the growth direct from the field. In this year of Jubilee, each of you shall return to his holding. (Lev. 25:8–13)

The Jubilee, which crowns seven seven-year shemitta cycles, is a kind of super-sabbatical year. In addition to ceasing agricultural work, Hebrew slaves go free and every person returns to his ancestral holdings – meaning the piece of land that his family held when Joshua divided up the Land of Israel on entering the land three thousand years ago. Whatever gains and losses in land holdings may have occurred over the previous fifty years, whether through good or bad luck, alacrity or laziness, talent or foolishness, were all erased. There was a society-wide reset as each family returned to its original patrimony. Accumulated socioeconomic advantages could not be passed down indefinitely to one's descendants; with the restoration of land, each family was returned to an original position of dignity and opportunity.

The shemitta and Jubilee commandments are immensely radical. They legislate a septennial time-out in Jewish economic life, a year of spiritual renewal, a holiday for the land, a yearlong ceasefire in the economic struggle of all against all, an abolition of many of the rights of private property, a leveling of rich and poor, man and beast, earth and earth-dwellers, an amnesty on debt and, every half-century, a reset on the vicissitudes of the free market. These mitzvot represent a periodic challenge to the whole socioeconomic order. As Gerald Blidstein put it in an important article: "We have here more than the commonplace struggle between a radical religious demand and an unconsenting world. Rather, we have here an institution that contests the legitimacy of that world."[2]

So it is not surprising that the history of these commandments has been marked by conflict between their exacting requirements and the demands of economic reality. Indeed, it is remarkable that shemitta was observed as diligently and for as long as it was. There is strong evidence that the sabbatical for the land was observed throughout the Second Temple period. At the famous assembly described by Nehemiah on their return to Israel in 516 BCE, the Jews took upon themselves the observance of shemitta as a central element of their renewed commitment to the covenant (Neh. 10:32). Among the many sources testifying that they indeed kept shemitta is an account in Josephus' *Antiquities* of Alexander

2. Gerald Jacob Blidstein, "Man and Nature in the Sabbatical Year," *Tradition* 9, no. 4 (1966): 50.

the Great reaching Jerusalem and acceding to the high priest's request that the Jews be exempt from paying tribute during the sabbatical year, when they did not work the land.[3] Numerous tannaitic sources attest that Jews in Israel continued to observe shemitta for centuries after the destruction of Jerusalem by the Romans. After most Jews were exiled, shemitta of the land (*shemittat karkaot*) brought ever-greater economic hardships for the remaining Jews in the Land of Israel and despite various rabbinic leniencies, eventually lapsed around the fifth century. With the rise of a vibrant Jewish community in Safed, northern Israel, in the sixteenth century, shemitta once again became a live issue. A celebrated dispute occurred in the shemitta year of 1532 between the two greatest authorities of the Safed community, Rabbi Yosef Karo and Rabbi Moshe di Trani (known as Mabit), about the sabbatical year status of produce grown on land owned by non-Jews. The argument enjoyed a long afterlife, and Rabbi Karo's view became a cornerstone of Rav Kook's position nearly four hundred years later.

The remission of debts (*shemittat kesafim*), though technically binding inside and outside Israel, became largely moot from the first century BCE. Hillel the Elder saw that people were doing exactly what the Torah had warned them not to do: they were withholding loans in the run-up to the shemitta year. The poor suffered most from people's reluctance to lend them money, an unintended consequence of a law that was meant to help them. So Hillel instituted the famous *prozbul* enactment, which handed over the responsibility for outstanding debts to the courts, which, as a public authority, were allowed to collect debts. Thus, observance of *shemittat kesafim* may be avoided. As for the Jubilee, according to most traditional sources, its practice ceased sometime during the First Temple period, when two and a half of the twelve tribes were exiled,[4] and there is some doubt as to whether the Jubilee was ever properly observed.

Maimonides writes, in his account of the messianic era at the end of the *Mishneh Torah*, that among the many enactments to be expected of the Messiah, he will "cause the *shemittot* and the Jubilees to be observed

---

3. Josephus, *Antiquities* 11:338, quoted in *Encyclopaedia Judaica* 14:583.
4. Arakhin 32b.

as they are commanded in the Torah,"[5] clearly implying that they will not be fully observed until the Messiah comes. Rav Kook also suggests this in *Shabbat HaAretz*. Only then will the socioeconomic order make space to fully honor these mitzvot, which radically question its legitimacy. The *heter mekhira* controversy has been the main modern arena for this clash between the demands of shemitta and the exigencies of economic life and the principal modern test of the pre-messianic viability of shemitta. The controversy was inextricably bound up with the life, times, and thought of Rabbi Abraham Isaac Kook.

LIFE OF RAV KOOK[6]

Rabbi Abraham Isaac Kook was born in Grieva, a small town in Lithuania, in 1865. His father, Shlomo Zalman HaCohen Kook, was descended from a distinguished rabbinical family and studied at the Volozhin yeshiva, the greatest academy of talmudic learning and piety in nineteenth-century Europe. His mother, Perel Zlota, came from a Chabad Hasidic family. She had imbibed the mystical passion of Hasidism and maintained her connection to Chabad after her marriage. When the third Lubavitcher rebbe, Menachem Mendel Schneerson, died in 1866, she received a button and some threads from his cloak, which she sewed into the skullcap of her eldest son, Abraham Isaac. Later in life, Rav Kook remarked to one of his students that his parents used to argue whether he would become an ascetic Mitnagdic rabbi in the Volozhin mold or a Hasidic master. In any event, he was able to integrate both models into his complex and multifaceted personality.

Abraham Isaac was recognized early on as a prodigy of rabbinic learning. From a young age, he studied alone or with private tutors, soon mastering the Talmud and Jewish law. At age fifteen, he left home to study in the *beit midrash* of Litsin, where he encountered *maskilim*

5. Maimonides, *Mishneh Torah, Hilkhot Melakhim UMilḥemoteihem* 11:1.
6. I was fortunate to benefit from prepublication access to Yehudah Mirsky's outstanding biography of Rav Kook, which surpasses previous attempts to write about Rav Kook's life. See Mirsky, *Rav Kook: Mystic in a Time of Revolution* (New Haven, CT: Yale University Press, 2014). This biographical sketch is highly indebted to Mirsky's book, and statements in this section that are not otherwise attributed may be assumed to be from there.

(Jews who had absorbed the ideas of the European Enlightenment). He began to write verse and speak rich and precise grammatical Hebrew like a *maskil*. He then spent a year and a half studying in the Volozhin yeshiva, where he stood out for his learning and piety. Among Kook's fellow students at Volozhin were Micha Yosef Berdyczewski, who became a leading figure of Hebrew literature, and Chaim Nachman Bialik, later the national poet of Israel.

After Volozhin, Abraham Isaac married Batsheva Rabinowitz-Teomim. Compelled by poverty to seek a rabbinical position, he found employment as rabbi of Zoimel, a small town near the border with Latvia. In 1889, his wife died of pneumonia, leaving a baby daughter. Though devastated by grief, he quickly remarried; his second marriage was to his wife's cousin, with whom he had three more children. However, he continued to mourn his first wife for years afterward. During this period, he studied kabbala intensively with the renowned scholar Rabbi Shlomo Elyashiv.

In 1896, Kook became rabbi of Boisk, a city of some ten thousand people. Boisk had a relatively well-off and educated Jewish community. During this period, Rav Kook expanded his studies of literature and philosophy. Though the sources of his secular education are unclear, we know that he was familiar with the main currents of modern European thought, citing Spinoza, Kant, Schopenhauer, and Nietzsche, among others, in his writings.

Throughout the 1890s, he sought a Jewish language in which to give expression to his rich inner world. He began a commentary on the *Ein Yaakov*, a sixteenth-century compilation of the aggadic (nonlegal) parts of the Talmud. The aggada, being less systematic and structured than the halakhic parts of the Talmud, allowed for a more expressive religious vocabulary. Rav Kook was also engaged with the Musar controversy, which was shaking the Eastern European yeshivot at that time. Musar was a movement of ethical revival, pioneered by Rabbi Israel Salanter, but it attracted criticism for the excesses of emotional exhortation and self-criticism of its followers. Rav Kook saw something valuable in the intense inwardness of Musar but believed that for it to be most effective, Musar needed to be studied from a text that one wrote oneself from the teachings nearest to one's soul.

After 1896, when Theodor Herzl convened the First Zionist Congress in Basel, the possibilities of a political return to Zion began to preoccupy Rav Kook. Between 1901 and 1904, he published a series of essays through which he emerged as a supporter of Jewish nationalism, albeit with some qualifications. Rav Kook was disturbed by the antireligious impulse that he saw in the nascent Zionist movement and argued that if Zionism remained divorced from religion, it would degenerate into mere nationalistic chauvinism.

In 1902, Yoel Moshe Salomon, a leading figure in the nascent Jewish settlements in Palestine, visited Boisk, seeking a new rabbi for Jaffa, an ancient town with a rapidly growing Jewish population that was becoming the urban hub of the new agricultural communities. Salomon was much taken with Rav Kook, and, shortly after his visit, the Jaffa search committee offered Rav Kook the post. Despite his growing stature in the European rabbinate and Jaffa's reputation as "a place of desolate sin," he accepted the opportunity to play a formative role in the development of the Jewish community in Israel. He arrived in Jaffa on May 13, 1904.

The Jewish population in the Land of Israel at that time was divided into two opposing groups. One group was the Old Yishuv, comprising staunchly traditional Orthodox Jews who had emigrated during the nineteenth century for religious reasons – to study Torah and pray in the Holy Land. This community did not see itself as responsible for the economic and physical building of the land but subsisted almost entirely on a system of donations from Jews in the Diaspora, known as the *ḥaluka*. The other group comprised Zionist pioneers of the New Yishuv. The wave of immigration beginning in 1882 known as the First Aliyah had been predominantly religious, but the Second Aliyah, beginning in 1904, was composed mainly of secular immigrants motivated by a mixture of Marxism, social democracy, Nietzschean notions of self-realization, and rebellion against Jewish tradition and the pioneers' bourgeois family backgrounds. Their goal was to create "normal" economic structures, thriving independently and supporting themselves by their own labor. The Old Yishuv regarded the pioneers of the New Yishuv as dangerous heretics dedicated to destroying traditional Jewish life. The New Yishuv, for its part, regarded the Old as primitive throwbacks to everything they hated about Diaspora Jewish life. David Ben-

Gurion, who arrived with the Second Aliyah, charged that the leaders of the Old Yishuv "annihilate every free idea and crush every attempt for liberation.... This sector is dead and buried [and is] a population of obscurantists and schnorrers."[7] Spanning the chasm between these factions became a defining task of Rav Kook's life.

Rav Kook admired the pioneers' dedication and self-sacrifice in building the country and was excited by the redemptive possibilities of Jewish farmers planting the Land of Israel. Soon after his arrival, he toured the surrounding agricultural settlements, including Rishon LeTzion, Nes Tziona, and Gedera, remarking to a friend: "I could kiss every stone of this holy land." He also shared much of the new immigrants' critique of the Old Yishuv, writing that "the vitality of the New Yishuv...cannot bear to see the hunched back, the drawn and melancholy face, that summons despair and faintness of heart, the vague eyes and the despair and hatred of life behind them."[8]

At the same time, Rav Kook was pained by the pioneers' rejection of Jewish tradition, He crystallized his ambivalence in a famous essay, "The Present Generation," in which he wrote: "Our generation is wondrous, a generation full of puzzlement. One is hard-pressed to find anything like it in all our history. It is composed of opposites, darkness and light groping about in confusion. It is low and degraded, and great and exalted; it is entirely guilty and entirely innocent."[9] He dreamed of a synthesis between the vitality of the New Yishuv and the commitment to tradition of the Old Yishuv. Rav Kook attempted to engage the secular writers and artists who were his neighbors in the Neve Tzedek area of Jaffa, with mixed success. Shai Agnon, who later won the Nobel Prize for Literature, had a regular *ḥavruta* with Rav Kook and became a lifelong admirer; Yosef Chaim Brenner, a mordant and saturnine observer of Diaspora Jewish life and regarded by many of his contemporaries as a sort of secular saint, was more guarded, praising Rav Kook as a "stormy

---

7. David Ben-Gurion, "On the Question of the Old Yishuv," *Ha'aḥdut* (1910): 2, quoted in Benjamin Ish-Shalom, *Rav Avraham Itzhak HaCohen Kook: Between Rationalism and Mysticism*, trans. Ora Wiskind-Elper (Albany, NY: SUNY Press, 1993), 15.
8. *Iggerot HaRe'aya* 1:185, quoted in Ish-Shalom, *Rav Avraham*, 21.
9. "Hador," in *Eder HaYakar* (Jerusalem: Mossad HaRav Kook, 1967), 108.

and yearning soul" but scorning the "confused assumptions and untenable visions" of the latter's religious worldview.[10]

Shabbat HaAretz was written amid the controversy about shemitta observance that shook the Yishuv in 1909. The roots of the dispute lay back in 1888, the first shemitta year after the beginning of the First Aliyah. This wave of immigration, beginning in 1882, brought some 60,000 mostly religious Jews from Eastern Europe to live in the Yishuv. Unlike the traditionalists of the Old Yishuv, who subsisted on charitable donations from Europe, the newcomers worked the land. They endured poverty, starvation, malaria, and horrific rates of infant mortality as they struggled to eke out a living from agriculture.

With the advent of the shemitta of 1888–89, it was clear to many of the pioneers that observing the sabbatical year as commanded in the Bible would be economically ruinous and would likely lead to the extinction of the nascent agricultural settlements.[11] Moreover, most of these settlements were supported by Baron Edmond de Rothschild, whose administrators exercised close control over all aspects of community life. These officials, imbued with French colonialist ideals of enlightened efficiency, would not countenance their subjects taking a year off from their work.[12] For a solution, the neophyte farmers appealed to European rabbis, including Rabbi Shmuel Mohilever, who ruled that they might continue to work the land in the sabbatical year, provided that the land was sold to non-Jews for the duration of the shemitta. This leniency was patterned after the permission to sell *ḥametz*, leavened food, to non-Jews during Passover in order to avoid serious financial loss. It was endorsed

10. Yosef Chaim Brenner, in *Hapo'el Hatza'ir* 40 (1910), quoted in Ish-Shalom, *Rav Avraham*, 23.
11. A minority, however, especially in the village of Mazkeret Batya, determined to observe the biblical shemitta to the letter.
12. For a well-documented description of Rothschild's involvement in the 1888–89 shemitta controversy, see Simon Schama, *Two Rothschilds and the Land of Israel* (London, 1978), 99–103. Schama argues that Rothschild himself approached Eastern European rabbis for a halakhic solution to the shemitta question. Schama's book gives a vivid account both of Rothschild's munificence toward the settlements and of his paternalistic methods of administration.

by Rabbi Yitzchak Elchanan Spektor of Kovno, the leading halakhic authority of the late nineteenth century.

The *heter mekhira*, as it became known, was seen as a temporary expedient. It was renewed for the shemitta years of 1895–96 and 1902–3, each time amid bitter criticism from the Old Yishuv, which was not engaged in agriculture and saw the *heter* as a specious device for avoiding a biblical commandment.

By the shemitta of 1909–10, the agrarian settlements had grown in scope and scale but still could not have survived the rigors of full shemitta observance. Moreover, they had begun to export agricultural produce. They would lose these markets through ceasing work for a year and would probably be unable to recover them. A further difference this time around was that the religious farmers of the First Aliyah had now been augmented by the secularists of the Second Aliyah, who had no intention of taking a year off in the shemitta.

Rav Kook's close identification with the pioneers led him to strongly endorse the *heter mekhira*. He argued in the face of opposition from rabbis in the Diaspora that only through direct knowledge of the suffering and self-sacrifice of the Zionist farmers could one truly understand what was at stake. Furthermore, the very viability of Judaism in the renewed Yishuv was on the line. If the halakha could provide no solution to the most pressing existential needs of the farmers, they would turn their backs on Judaism in droves. He argued that if the rabbis showed themselves to be oblivious to the most basic needs of life, the result would be the destruction of Torah and the abandonment of mitzvot.

In the summer of 1909, Rav Kook threw himself into educational activity around the issue of shemitta in general and the *heter mekhira* in particular, culminating in the composition of *Shabbat HaAretz*, a densely argued 120-page work (written in just a week) that provided the most thorough, learned, and audacious justification for the *heter* that had ever been made.

The publication of *Shabbat HaAretz* ratcheted the controversy up to a new level. Rav Kook's most determined and prominent adversary was Rav Yaakov David Willowsky (known as the "Ridbaz"), the rabbi of Safed, who had emigrated from Chicago in 1905. The Ridbaz opined that the sale of the *heter mekhira* was entirely fictional and made no difference to the status of the land. He purchased a small plot of land in the Galilee on the eve of the 1909–10 shemitta just so that he could let it lie fallow. He accused Rav Kook of having been duped by his sympathy for the secular settlers into supporting the blatant transgression of one of the Torah's commandments. The two continued a polemical correspondence almost until the Ridbaz's death, in 1913. Rav Kook urged the Ridbaz to see that this was the generation that the Zohar called "good within but rotten without," which would build the material basis for redemption and required the support of rabbinic leaders to accomplish. The Ridbaz, a Lithuanian legal scholar to the core, saw only an egregious violation of the integrity of the Torah and was "unmoved by mystical attempts to find hidden light in everyone and everything."[13] Rav Kook refused to return in kind the often personal attacks of his detractors. He reaffirmed his belief that he and his critics were both arguing *leshem shamayim* – for the sake of vital religious principles.

In November 1913, Rav Kook embarked on his most ambitious practical effort to build bridges to the New Yishuv. Together with a small group of rabbis, including Yosef Chaim Sonnenfeld, the leading authority of the Old Yishuv at the time, he set out on a monthlong trip to visit all the agricultural communities in the center and north of the country. The goals of the trip were to engage the pioneers in dialogue and strengthen Jewish education and the mitzvot connected to the land (tithes, first fruits, and so on). The rabbis met with enthusiastic responses in more traditional First Aliyah settlements such as Zikhron Yaakov and Hadera but with more varied receptions in the strongholds of the Second Aliyah. In Merhavia, the workers virtually chased the rabbis out of the communal kitchen. Rav Kook calmly responded: "We have not come to influence you but rather to be influenced by your tremendous sacrifice on behalf of the Land of Israel."[14] At Poriya, overlooking the Sea of Galilee, Rav Kook took off his black coat and donned a watchman's cloak

13. Mirsky, *Rav Kook*, 76.
14. This is a well-known anecdote, quoted in a film about Rav Kook's life that is shown at Beit HaRav, his house in Jerusalem. I have not been able to find a written source. The story of Rav Kook's 1913 journey is recounted in detail in Yonatan Binyamin Halevi Horowitz, *Eleh Masei* (Jerusalem: Oraita, 2001). Horowitz accompanied Rav Kook on the trip and wrote his account in 1915.

and head-scarf to dance with the pioneers, demonstrating his sense of kinship with them, beneath their very different garbs.[15] The tour concluded with a stop in Safed, where Rav Kook made a condolence visit to the widow of the Ridbaz, who had recently died.

In the summer of 1914, when Rav Kook and his wife were traveling to the Agudat Yisrael conference in Germany, the First World War broke out. The Kooks took refuge for a year and a half in Saint Gallen, Switzerland, where Rav Kook met David Cohen (known as "the Nazir" because he had sworn not to cut his hair or drink wine), a philosophy student who later became Rav Kook's closest disciple. In search of a spiritual master, Cohen had traveled to meet Rav Kook. After several hours of philosophical discussion, Cohen had been unconvinced as to whether this was indeed his rebbe, but the next morning, when he overheard Rav Kook praying, he knew that he had found what he had sought. "I listened," he later wrote, "and I was turned upside-down and became a different man."

In January 1916, Rav Kook moved to London to become rabbi of the Machzikei Hadath Orthodox synagogue on Brick Lane, in the East End. There, Rav Kook gathered an eclectic community of Hasidim, tailors, intellectuals, and East End radicals. He signed numerous rabbinic-ordination certificates to save young Jews from conscription (earning a stern warning from Scotland Yard). He also found time to frequent the National Gallery, becoming especially fond of Rembrandt. Rav Kook confided in an interview to the *Jewish Chronicle* that Rembrandt was one of the few tzaddikim who was privileged to see in this world the pure light that, according to a midrash, God stored up for the righteous in the world to come.[16]

While in London, Rav Kook became involved in public debates around the Balfour Declaration, championing the centrality of the Land of Israel in Judaism against those assimilated British Jews who opined

15. This story is related in a letter dated September 1972, from Avraham Rosenblatt, a Tel Aviv accountant who had been present at Poriya during Rav Kook's 1913 visit, to Rabbi Yisrael Meir Lau, then chief rabbi of Tel Aviv. A facsimile of the letter is published in the sourcebook *Le'an Atah Holekh* (Jerusalem: Beit HaRav Kook, 2013).
16. Avram Melnikoff, "Rav Kook on Art," *Jewish Chronicle*, September 13, 1935.

that the idea of Jewish nationhood was a biblical anachronism. The announcement of the declaration, in November 1917, electrified the religious Jewish world and roused Rav Kook to "old-new thoughts of spiritual and practical work" that he had dreamed of accomplishing in Israel. As the war drew to a close, he began to seek ways to return home. At the same time, the secular Zionists were looking for a reasonable rabbi to confer religious legitimacy on Zionism; and moderate rabbis in Jerusalem, led by Zvi Pesach Frank, were attempting to find a leader who would be a counterweight to the ultra-Orthodox. These different search paths converged on Rav Kook, who was offered the position of chief rabbi of Jerusalem in 1919. He returned to the holy city in late August of that year to assume the role.

In the postwar Yishuv, nation-building supplanted ideological discussion as the focus of the Jewish communities. As Yehudah Mirsky astutely points out, this shift left Rav Kook at a disadvantage. His unique ability to intellectually bridge and unite various Jewish groups far outstripped his skills in building or running organizations. He never developed a political or cultural base that could hold its own in the evolving ecosystem of Jewish institutions that became the nucleus of the future state. He envisioned the creation of a chief rabbinate that would lead the spiritual renaissance of the Jewish people in its land and take its place alongside the Hebrew University, the Zionist Executive, and other national institutions in waiting.

The secular Zionists supported an altogether more modest chief rabbinate that would deliver religious services and dampen intra-Jewish tensions while remaining firmly under the secular Zionists' control. The British – who were, by then, running the country – wanted a single Jewish address to turn to for religious matters (though they ended up with two – one Ashkenazi and one Sephardi); they convened an assembly that unanimously voted in Rav Kook as first chief rabbi of Palestine, in February 1921. The Old Yishuv, still deeply suspicious of Rav Kook's unconventional views and outreach to the secular, refused to recognize the chief rabbinate's authority. Mirsky summarizes the theory and practice of Rav Kook's chief rabbinate: "He sought to restore the great lawmaking bodies of classical Judaism and realize Maimonides' vision of halakhic constitutionalism, and what he got was a chronically underfunded, politically orphaned clerical bureaucracy."[17]

In his final years, Rav Kook was revered by the Yishuv (with the exception of some ultra-Orthodox zealots who continued to revile him until his death and, indeed, after it) as a spiritual giant. He was a courageous moral voice who spoke out against the British authority's supine inaction during the 1929 massacres of Jews by Arabs and against the British restrictions on Jews praying at the Western Wall. He championed the innocence of Abraham Stavsky and Abba Achimeir, Revisionist Zionists who were accused of murdering the Labor Zionist leader Chaim Arlosoroff in 1933, a cause célèbre that convulsed the whole Yishuv; Stavsky and Achimeir were subsequently acquitted.

Rav Kook died of cancer on September 1, 1935. Memorial services were held for him all over Palestine and in Jewish communities around the world. At one gathering, Rabbi Meir Bar-Ilan (a Religious Zionist leader and son of the Netziv, Rav Kook's *rosh yeshiva* in Volozhin) eulogized him: "Rav Kook loved the Jewish people, the way only a father can love his children. Nobody is left after him who will love the nation that fiercely.... He understood his people, the situation of the generation and its life conditions, and that is why he forgave them everything."

THOUGHT OF RAV KOOK

Rav Kook was one of the most important and influential Jewish thinkers of all time. His ideas are indispensable for understanding the state of Israeli politics and religion today. His immense body of writings includes profound and often startlingly original treatments of all the subjects that traditional Jewish thinkers concerned themselves with (as well as many that they did not), including God, revelation, Torah, commandments, halakha, prayer, personal authenticity, art, science, evolution, socialism, nationalism, universalism, and messianism. In the face of this vast work, the following overview will merely summarize the areas of his thinking that are most relevant for understanding Rav Kook's thought about shemitta.

17. Mirsky, *Rav Kook*, 235.

Kabbala

Scholars generally agree that kabbalistic mysticism was the backbone of Rav Kook's worldview (although they disagree over the extent to which his ideas were also influenced by the European thinking of his time).[18] Rav Kook saw the universe as permeated with divine light. In the words of a classic passage from the Zohar, which he often quoted: "There is no place that is empty of Him, either above or below" (*Tikunei HaZohar* 59). Godliness animates all ideas, people, and creatures. "There is a spark of divine light in all things."[19]

This vision was based on the teachings of Lurianic kabbala, the masterly systematization of Jewish mysticism achieved by Rabbi Isaac Luria (1534–72) and his students. Lurianic kabbala teaches that at the moment of Creation, infinite divine light was poured into "vessels," which, unable to withstand the intensity, shattered, scattering fragments of divine light everywhere. Much of the light became encased in *kelipot* – impure husks and shells that captured the sparks and prevented them from shining. This is the world we live in, full of trapped fragments of light. The goal of Jewish spiritual service – particularly the service of the tzaddikim, the truly righteous – is to identify, liberate, and raise up the hidden sparks.

For Rav Kook, the divine light of truth could be found almost anywhere: "This concept of tolerance is aware that there is a spark of divine light in all things, that the inner spark of divine light shines in all the different religions, as so many different pedagogics for the culture of humanity, to improve the spiritual and material existence, the present and future of the individual and of society."[20] To be sure, he was no

18. Benjamin Ish-Shalom, *Rav Avraham*, has done notable work in identifying sources for Rav Kook's thought in Western philosophy. Paul Franks gives a thorough genealogy of F.W.J. Schelling's influence on Rav Kook in his article "Mythology, Essence, and Form: Schelling's Jewish Reception in the Nineteenth Century," *International Journal of Philosophy and Theology*, 80 (2019), 71–89. Yosef Avivi's masterly four-volume study, *Kabbalat HaRe'aya* (Jerusalem, 2017), establishes beyond doubt the grounding of Rav Kook's thinking in Lurianic kabbala.
19. "Concerning the Conflict of Beliefs and Opinions," in *Abraham Isaac Kook*, trans. Ben Zion Bokser (Mahwah, NJ: Paulist Press, 1978), 273.
20. Ibid.

relativist, and he emphatically declared that divine light was most fully present in the Torah, the revelation nurtured by the Jewish people. But he regarded the opinion that there is no truth outside Torah as "a frightful blindness" and taught that "the heart must be filled with love for all."[21]

Secularism

Rav Kook's embrace of the secular pioneers must be understood in light of this worldview. These pioneers were rebels against tradition and deniers of core Jewish beliefs; yet Rav Kook saw in their love and self-sacrifice on behalf of the Jewish people and the Land of Israel a blazing fire of divine light. He believed that Providence had chosen them to be the agents for the rebuilding and renaissance of Jewish life. The socialist and secular-nationalist ideologies in which they clothed their passion were, for Rav Kook, *kelipot* that would eventually fall away.

This attitude was radical enough to earn him the enmity of Orthodox factions, who could see nothing but heresy in secular Zionism. But Rav Kook went even further. In a seminal essay, "The Souls of Chaos," Rav Kook implies that the idealistic rebels of the Second Aliyah were greater and closer to the divine light than many adherents of tradition: "The great idealists seek an order so firm and pure, beyond what may be found in the world of reality.... The souls inspired by the realm of chaos are greater than the souls whose affinity is with the established order. They are very great; they seek too much from existence, what is beyond their own faculties to assimilate. They seek a very great light."[22] The exalted stature and aspirations of such souls lead them into conflict with more prescribed and limited visions of goodness.

The pioneers' impatience with tradition manifested itself in chutzpah. In addition to being a Jewish folk characteristic, chutzpah is also a term of art with talmudic and kabbalistic antecedents. In "The Present Generation," Rav Kook wrote that the key to understanding the secularists was the strange talmudic statement from Mishna Sota 9:15, *be'ikveta demashiḥa ḥutzpa yasgei* ("In the time of the footsteps of the Messiah,

21. "The Moral Principles: Love," in Bokser, *Abraham Isaac Kook*, 135.
22. "The Souls of Chaos," in Bokser, *Abraham Isaac Kook*, 256.

chutzpah will grow").[23] Their rebellion against received ideas, norms, and behavior reflected a deeper attunement to the mighty messianic ideals that would be revealed in the imminent future.

For all the esteem in which he held the pioneers, Rav Kook was also grieved by their dismissal of tradition and believed that their idealism would fizzle and come to nothing if it remained divorced from the time-trodden paths to morality and holiness represented by the life of Torah and mitzvot. He was impelled to engage with them even where other rabbinic leaders were repelled. Explaining his position, he wrote at the end of "The Souls of Chaos":

> These passionate souls reveal their strength so that no fence can hold them back; and the weaklings of the established order, who are guided by balance and propriety, are too terrified to tolerate them.... But in truth, there is no need to be terrified.... Truly heroic spirits know that this force is one of the phenomena needed for the perfection of the world, for strengthening the power of the nation, of man, and of the world. Initially, this force represents the realm of the chaotic. But in the end, it will be taken from the wicked and turned over to the hands of the righteous.[24]

As one of the "truly heroic spirits," Rav Kook felt driven to bridge the old and new, secular and traditional, pioneers and pietists, to demonstrate the beauty and relevance of Judaism to the secularists and the great-souled nature of the secularists to the religious.

Nationalism and Zionism

Rav Kook's relationship to Zionism was passionately supportive, yet conditional. He believed that the flowering of Jewish life in the Land of Israel that Zionism had inspired was nothing less than the beginning of the messianic redemption. "So shall it be in our days," he wrote in a letter, "as a result of our strengthening of the growing Yishuv...the light

23. "Hador," 109.
24. "The Souls of Chaos," 258.

of redemption and salvation will flourish."[25] He (unlike some of his followers) did not attempt to predict how long the "beginning" would last but was certain that the physical rebuilding and planting being done by the Zionist pioneers would eventually serve as a basis for the spiritual renaissance and transformation of the Jewish people and the universal redemption of all humankind.

This view was highly unconventional at the time and differed markedly from the stands of the traditionalists of the Old Yishuv and also the mainstream Religious Zionists of the Mizrachi movement. For the traditionalists, Zionism was a heresy that violated the implicit contract of the exile set out in the classic passage of the "Three Oaths" (Talmud, Ketubot 110b–111a), according to which banishment from the Land of Israel was divine punishment and the Jewish people had no right to try to force an end to the exile before God made clear that the time had come. For Rabbi Yitzchak Reines (1839–1915), founder of the Mizrachi movement, on the other hand, Zionism was a welcome vehicle for national improvement that had nothing to do with messianism. He supported Zionism as a means to raise the people's dignity and standing and bring them to a happy life. Reines' approach smoothed the path of cooperation with the secular Zionists but disturbed Rav Kook, as it seemed to deny the clearly miraculous, proto-messianic character of the Jewish revival that Zionism had engendered.

His messianic commitments rendered Rav Kook's embrace of Zionism conditional. Jewish nationalism was not a good in itself but was valuable for the values and historical mission that it helped to realize. Rav Kook warned of the danger that nationalism without spiritual content would degenerate into hollow chauvinism. His early Eastern European writings on Zionism bore the imprint of Aḥad Ha'am, for whom ethics was the defining characteristic of the Jewish national spirit.

For the mature Rav Kook, however, the return to the Land of Israel made possible the fulfillment not merely of collective ethics but of holiness, which he understood as that which reveals the unity of things, in all their diversity. In contrast to the classical Jewish under-

25. Letter to Rav Yaakov David Willowsky (the Ridbaz); *Iggerot HaRe'aya* 1:348 (Jerusalem, 2002).

standing of holiness as separateness (e.g., "You shall be holy" [Lev. 19:2] is interpreted by the Sifrei as "you shall be separate"), Rav Kook viewed holiness holistically, as the interrelated harmony of all being. He wrote: "The sacred must be built on the foundation of the profane. The profane is the matter of the sacred, and the sacred is its form; the more powerful the matter, the more significant the form."[26] Holiness is achieved through the integration of the sacred and secular, rather than through their separation. This understanding has its antecedents in the Hasidic idea of *avoda begashmiyut,* serving God in the earthly physical world and, before that, in the declaration of the *Tikunei HaZohar*, quoted above: "There is no place that is empty of Him."

Holiness is present when the spiritual and the material are unified and the connections between them are made manifest. Only through the return of the Jewish people to its own land and the embrace of life in all its dimensions – including, crucially, the aspect of agriculture – could the people's holiness be realized and its spiritual character and mission be articulated. As Rav Kook wrote of the Jewish role in history, "We began to say something of immense importance among ourselves and to the entire world, but we have not yet finished it.... The truth is so rich that we stammer; our speech is still in exile.... In the course of time, we shall be able to express what we seek *with our entire being*."[27]

The most important things in the universe, then, were at stake in the Zionist farmers' struggles to survive by working the land in the Land of Israel. They were gaining a precious physical foothold that would one day lead to the full-fledged flowering of redemption. By returning to agricultural work, they were opening new pathways of holiness, and, as Rav Kook makes clear in the introduction to *Shabbat HaAretz,* the unique rhythm of economic life patterned by the laws of shemitta and *yovel* is a prominent part of the unique message that the Jewish people is called upon to articulate to the world.

---

26. *Orot HaKodesh* (Jerusalem: Mossad HaRav Kook, 1938, 1985), 1:148.
27. Quoted in Bokser, *Abraham Isaac Kook,* xix.

Socialism

A strong socialist ethos prevailed among the pioneers of the Second Aliyah, who arrived in Ottoman Palestine in 1904–14 and rapidly came to dominate the politics and culture of the Jewish settlement. Many, including Yosef Chaim Brenner and Micha Yosef Berdyczewski, had flirted with revolutionary movements in Russia before emigrating. Immigrants from the Second Aliyah invented the kibbutz, one of the most successful experiments ever in egalitarian communal living.[28]

Many of the central commandments of shemitta tend toward creating a more equal society. The requirements that all may come and eat what grows by itself in the fields during the sabbatical year, as well as that loans be forgiven, partially redress the disadvantages of the weak in the marketplace. At a number of places in the introduction to *Shabbat HaAretz*, Rav Kook strikes a note of pronounced suspicion about commerce, writing, for example, about "the conflict, compulsion, and pressure … that surround buying, selling, and acquiring things" and our "mundane lives, with their toil, anxiety, anger, and competition."

In his more sustained discussion of socialism, Rav Kook showed a large measure of sympathy with the movement's egalitarian goals, writing: "We do not sorrow if some quality of social justice can be constructed without mention of any spark of the divine because we know that the very aspiration for justice, in whatever form it has, is itself the most illuminating divine influence."[29]

While praising the passion for social justice in socialism, Rav Kook deplored the atheistic, historical materialist philosophy at the core of Marxism. Yet he was confident that eventually, the atheistic shell of socialism would crumble, revealing the divinely inspired ideals within:

> And if man wishes to build the general cosmological structure without any participation of spiritual influence but through calculations of materialistic necessity, we remain serene of heart, observing this child's construction, which builds the shell of life

28. The first kibbutz, Degania Alef, was founded in 1909 on the shores of the Sea of Galilee.
29. *Iggerot HaRe'aya* 1:45.

> when it does not know how to build life itself, and we draw closer and embrace therefore the connection to life and inner holiness. "I am the Lord your God who brought you out of the land of Egypt," not "who created the world."[30]

Rav Kook reminds us that God's self-identification with the Jewish people at Sinai is not as Creator but as the God who freed slaves from Egypt. Liberation of workers from oppression was a core Jewish spiritual value before Marxist historical materialism.

Particularism and Universalism

The interdependence of particular and universal is a vast theme in Rav Kook's writings; his teachings express a yearning for unity in which all details of life will be integrated into a broad holistic vision. For example: "The more the world develops and becomes whole, the more its parts are united and its organic quality becomes more apparent. The highest unification is the unification of the human's intellect and will with the entire universe, in general and in its particulars."[31]

The relationship between the particularity of Israel with the universality of all humanity is a crucial subtheme. Rav Kook's belief in the uniqueness of the people and the Land of Israel is evident throughout the introduction to *Shabbat HaAretz*; yet his equally strong universalist commitment is manifest frequently throughout his writings (e.g., "Love for all creatures must live in the heart and soul, love for every individual, and love for all the nations").[32] He repeatedly insists that a refined spiritual sensibility must rise above exclusive identification with any one group of people and "sing the song of all creation."

The introduction to *Shabbat HaAretz* uses phrases such as "the Jewish people's collective soul" and "this national treasure that is imprinted deep within us," which seem to suggest an essential difference between Jews and others. In fact, Rav Kook's position on this question is quite complex. The nature of the Jewish people's difference from other

30. Ibid.
31. *Orot HaKodesh* 2:441.
32. *Middot HaRe'aya, ahava* 5.

nations is a classic fault line in Jewish thought, whose key medieval protagonists were Yehuda Halevi and Maimonides. Halevi argues for an inherent, essential difference between Jews and non-Jews.[33] He did not believe that non-Jews could achieve prophecy. Maimonides, on the other hand, argued that the difference of the Jewish people consists in its having received the Torah, a unique manual of ethical training. Maimonides stated in a famous passage[34] that the highest levels of spiritual life are open and accessible to all who are willing to strive for them, Jewish or non-Jewish. In modern times, the Chabad-Lubavitch movement has espoused the essentialist position of Halevi, whereas Rabbi Joseph Dov Soloveitchik, leader of twentieth-century Modern Orthodoxy, adopted the educational position of Maimonides.

Rav Kook held a harmonistic position synthesizing Maimonides and Halevi; he followed Maimonides' view that individuals of all nations could reach the highest spiritual levels and Halevi's in asserting that the Jewish people possessed an inherent collective uniqueness: "From the perspective of select individuals, we know no distinction between peoples and languages and 'an alien who studies Torah is like a high priest.'... But our extolling of the community of Israel in general is due to the divine quality that is found in the *neshama* of the nation as a whole."[35]

In the introduction to *Shabbat HaAretz,* Rav Kook mostly uses the word *neshama* for "soul." This is the highest of three levels of soul that are commonly discussed by the kabbalists: *nefesh, ruaḥ,* and *neshama.* Although these three levels are usually applied to the individual, Rav Kook (following other kabbalists, including Rabbi Moshe Chaim Luzzatto)[36] also applied them to collectives and nations. The soul level of *neshama* in individuals is the power of thought and higher will; applied to the collective, it represents faith, ethics, religion, the quest for God, and the impulse to charity and justice. Rav Kook asserts here that the Jewish people's collective *neshama* is marked by an especially strong yearning for godliness.

---

33. E.g., *Kuzari* 1:27.
34. *Hilkhot Shemitta VeYovel* 13:12.
35. *Iggerot HaRe'aya* 1:70–71.
36. *Derekh HaShem,* part 2, ch. 4.

The ultimate goal of Israel's particularism is universal – the perfection of the whole world through the full realization of holiness in the life of the Jewish people.

Halakha and Aggada

A notable aspect of Rav Kook's quest to reveal the unity of all creation and phenomena was his passion to reconnect halakha and aggada. The Talmud is made up of roughly equal quantities of halakhic, legal discussion, and aggadic material, comprising stories, folklore, fantastic tales, midrashic retellings of the lives of biblical figures, philosophical reflection, ethical meditations, astronomical and other scientific observations, medical remedies, recipes, and much more. These divergent types of writing are thoroughly interwoven throughout the Talmud. Despite the editorial mixing of the two media, halakha and aggada are generally treated separately; indeed, in traditional yeshivot, aggada is often not treated at all but is skipped over as a distraction.

Rav Kook regretted this omission and called for a reintegration of the halakha with the aggada.[37] In his thinking, the halakha and aggada are frequently reflecting on common themes but in different cognitive modes. For example, the Talmud will shift from one register to another when the spiritual principle underlying a legal dispute calls forth a story as an illustration of its emotional depths. For him, the prevalent sense of separation between the two realms "removes the primary content of spiritual creativity; the tranquility that comes from inner unity."[38] In Rav Kook's view, to cut off norm from narrative, logic from imagination, rigor from reality, is to sever the unity of the mind and risk disturbing the creativity that flourishes through the free flow of ideas between different modes of thought.

The same idea was expressed lyrically by a contemporary of Rav Kook's, the poet Chaim Nachman Bialik, who wrote:

> Halakhah and aggadah are two things that are really one: two sides of a single shield.... Halakhah is the crystallization, the ultimate

37. *Orot HaKodesh* 1:25.
38. Ibid.

> and inevitable quintessence of aggadah; aggadah is the content of halakhah. Aggadah is the plaintive voice of the heart's yearning as it wings its way to its haven; halakhah is the resting place, where, for a moment, the yearning is satisfied and stilled. As a dream seeks its fulfillment in interpretation, as will in action, as thought in speech, as flower in fruit – so halakhah in aggadah.[39]

The relationship between the introduction to *Shabbat HaAretz* and the main body of the book is an example of this project of integration. The main text of *Shabbat HaAretz* is a 120-page halakhic argument in favor of the *heter mekhira* leniency that permitted selling parts of the Land of Israel to non-Jews in the shemitta year so as to avoid observing many of the stringent shemitta laws. As well as arguing for the *heter*, however, Rav Kook endeavored to educate about the importance of shemitta. This was the purpose of the non-halakhic introduction to *Shabbat HaAretz*, which discusses the socioeconomic, philosophical, and mystical significance of shemitta. By presenting here both the introduction to *Shabbat HaAretz* and excerpts from Rav Kook's halakhic arguments, I hope to show the profound connections between these contrasting elements and their mutually supporting role in achieving Rav Kook's purposes.

THE ARGUMENT OF *SHABBAT HAARETZ*

The halakhic content of *Shabbat HaAretz* was bold and innovative. Indeed, one of the book's novel features was that it was explicitly innovative. Rav Kook was not content to present the *heter mekhira* as a seamless evolution of Jewish law; unusually for a halakhic innovator, he stressed that he was proposing something new, arguing that the resettlement of the Land of Israel was a sufficiently radical development to require novel halakhic treatment:

> The sabbatical dispensation by a permit of sale on which we rely was never used and does not appear to have been relied upon by the early sages, of blessed memory, at the time of the Second

39. Haim Nahman Bialik, "Halachah and Aggadah," trans. by Leon Simon, in Bialik, *Revealment and Concealment: Five Essays* (Jerusalem: Ibis Editions, 2000), 46.

> Temple, in all the days of the sages of the Jerusalem Talmud, nor when the population continued to live in the Land of Israel afterward.... This is not surprising; in the early generations, the need was not so pressing.... Whenever there was no pressing need, the sages did not want to publicize dispensations based on legal fiction, following the maxim "It is the glory of the Lord to conceal a matter" (Prov. 25:2).... In the early days, when Jews lived primarily by working the land for sustenance, it was possible to observe the sanctity of the sabbatical year according to the details of the law without any dispensation; but in our days, when the existence of the community depends on commerce in the produce and crops of the agricultural settlements and the effect of preventing commerce would also lead to the destruction of future stability – under these circumstances, it is certainly our obligation to introduce the dispensation by way of sale of the land.[40]

Rav Kook alludes to the discretion with which halakhic authorities usually introduce innovation ("It is the glory of the Lord to conceal a matter"). This approach would not do in the present case, he argued. In the new situation – where the community subsisted by commerce in agricultural produce, including for export – it was imperative to introduce the dispensation of selling the land, and to do so publicly, to demonstrate the halakha's responsiveness to the changed reality.

Rav Kook addressed four basic issues in his argument for the *heter*: (1) whether the sabbatical year is a rabbinic prohibition (rather than a biblical prohibition) in contemporary times; (2) whether non-Jewish acquisition of land in the Land of Israel suspends its sanctity; (3) whether it is, in fact, permissible to sell land in the Land of Israel to a non-Jew; and (4) whether such a fictional sale has enough validity to actually effect the suspension of the sanctity of the land.

40. Rabbi Abraham Isaac Kook, *Shabbat HaAretz* (Hebrew) (Jerusalem: Mossad HaRav Kook, 1993), 113–15. Citations of *Shabbat HaAretz* in subsequent footnotes refer to this edition..

Is Shemitta a Rabbinic or Torah Prohibition in Our Times?

In order to set aside shemitta by selling the land, it was essential for Rav Kook to establish that shemitta in post-Temple times is of weaker rabbinic authority (*miderabanan*) rather than having the force of a Torah law (*mide'oraita*). This question had been extensively debated over centuries, and there were three major opinions:

1. Shemitta today has the force of a Torah law; Rabbi Yosef Karo, author of the *Shulḥan Arukh,* maintained that this was the opinion of Maimonides[41] (although Maimonides' text clearly allows for the opposite interpretation).
2. Shemitta today has the force of a rabbinic law. This was the most widely held opinion.[42] There were two main reasons given in the talmudic sources as to why this should be so. The first, attributed to R. Yehuda HaNasi, was that shemitta and *yovel,* the Jubilee year, were intimately connected. Jubilee is no longer observed, so the shemitta cannot be fully observed, either: "When the Jubilee was in operation, shemitta was in practice on the authority of the Torah; now that the Jubilee is not in operation, shemitta is practiced as a rabbinic ordinance."[43] The Jubilee is practiced, according to the Talmud, "when all the land's inhabitants are living there." Its practice ceased during the First Temple period, when two and a half of the tribes were exiled.[44] The other reason is that the agricultural laws in general are not in force during the post-Temple period.
3. Shemitta today does not even have rabbinic force but is a *midat ḥasidut* (supra-legal standard of piety). This was the view of the

41. Based on a reading of Maimonides, *Mishneh Torah, Hilkhot Shemitta VeYovel* 10:9, in Karo's *Kesef Mishneh* commentary, ad loc. However, in Rabbi Karo's subsequent *Beit Yosef* commentary on *Tur, Yoreh Deah* 331, he attributes to Maimonides the view that shemitta in our time is of rabbinic authority. On Maimonides' opinion, see p. 122, note 76 to the halakhic sections of *Shabbat HaAretz,* translated below.
42. See, e.g., Tur, *Yoreh De'ah* 331; Ritva, Rashba, and *Sefer HaḤinukh* also held this opinion.
43. Y. Shevi'it 10:2.
44. Ibid.; Arakhin 32b.

Provençal scholars Rabbi Zeraḥaya Halevi[45] (Razah) and Rabbi Avraham ben David of Posquières (Ravad).

Rav Kook reviewed the extensive halakhic sources and argued compellingly that (2) was correct.[46] He placed special emphasis on the opinion of R. Yehuda HaNasi, to whom the Talmud attributes the view that shemitta in our times is of rabbinic authority, as well as a number of other leniencies regarding the sabbatical year. R. Yehuda ruled, for example, that we cry out for rain during a drought in the shemitta year, even though agriculture is supposed to be suspended, "out of consideration for the livelihood of others."[47] Who are these "others" for whom we pray, the Talmud asks. R. Yehuda answers that they are the sinners who are violating the laws of shemitta! Underlining R. Yehuda's compassion toward transgressors of shemitta, the Talmud recounts, "A barber was suspected regarding sabbatical year produce. He was brought before R. Yehuda HaNasi. R. Yehuda HaNasi said to them: 'And what can the poor man do? He did it for the sake of his life.'"[48] Rav Kook explicitly associates himself with R. Yehuda's approach that includes the transgressors in his halakhic considerations, seeing him as a precedent for Rav Kook's own inclusivist position.

Having argued compellingly for R. Yehuda HaNasi's view that shemitta observance in our times is based on rabbinic authority, Rav Kook asked an interesting question: If the obligation to keep shemitta does not have the force of a Torah law, why did the rabbis establish it as even a rabbinic obligation? Why not adopt the third option, that shemitta in our times has no normative force at all? His striking answer is that the

45. The opinion of Razah is cited by *Sefer HaTerumot*, 55:4; Meiri, *Sefer Magen Avot*, 15. Recently, it was taken up and adopted by the Conservative halakhic writer Rabbi David Golinkin.

46. See the excerpt from the discussion in this volume, pp. 94–99, in which Rav Kook analyzes the principal relevant sources from the Babylonian Talmud: Moed Katan 2b and Gittin 36b.

47. Y. Taanit 3:1. R. Yehuda's compassionate understanding of shemitta transgressors is implicitly connected to his view that shemitta in our times is of rabbinic authority; a Torah command allows far less room for flexibility than a rabbinic ruling.

48. Ibid.

rabbis instituted it as a memorial of the full shemitta: "Its performance is primarily as a remembrance."[49] Keeping shemitta in our times is, among other things, an educational tool for keeping alive the ideal of what it could and should one day be. This leads Rav Kook to the remarkable idea that these educational goals can also be accomplished by marking one's avoidance of shemitta observance – for example, through the *heter mekhira*: "Since the evasion is carried out according to the prescriptions of the law, it constitutes a remembrance of the precept so that the law will not be forgotten, and when the time comes again for them to observe the biblical law, all the laws will be known."[50] Through the *heter mekhira*, shemitta is more honored in the breach than the observance.

Does Non-Jewish Acquisition of the Land Suspend Its Sanctity?

The question of whether selling the land to non-Jews does, in fact, suspend the holiness of the land was debated in sixteenth-century Safed by Rabbi Yosef Karo and Rabbi Moshe di Trani.[51] The specific question at issue then was whether crops grown by non-Jewish farmers during the shemitta year required the separation of tithes. Rabbi di Trani ruled that they did not, reasoning that such produce possesses the holiness of the shemitta year and is therefore *hefker*, ownerless, and as such not subject to tithes. Rabbi Karo responded that the talmudic concept, "the acquisition of the land by a non-Jew does not suspend its sanctity," applied only when a Jew subsequently reacquired the land or a Jew gathered the produce. In all other cases, he argued, the acquisition of the land

49. *Shabbat HaAretz*, 112. This is reminiscent of the midrash from Sifrei Deuteronomy, which taught that the reason for observing the commandments in exile was reminders or "as road markers," an idea that was adopted by Nahmanides in his Torah commentary.

50. Ibid.

51. Rabbi Yosef Karo, *Responsa Avkat Rokhel*, secs. 22–25. For a modern discussion of this debate, see David Tamar, "HaMaḥoket BiTzefat BeInyanei Shemitta UMaasrot," *HaMaayan* 35 (1995): 29. I have also benefited from a fascinating essay by Rabbi Benjamin Elton, "Is the Sanctity of the Land of Israel Alienable? The Debate between R. Yosef Karo and R. Moshe di Trani," in *Am Mekadeshei Shevi'i: A Collection of Teshuvot and Essays on Shemitah*, ed. Daniel R. Goodman (New York: Lindenbaum Center for Halakhic Studies, 2014). See the excerpt from section 11 of *Shabbat HaAretz*, translated below, for some of Rav Kook's discussion of this issue.

by a non-Jew suspended its sanctity. Rabbi Karo argued, in effect, that the sanctity of the land as applied to the agricultural commandments is not an absolute, objective category but a normative one and applies, as do most of the other commandments, to Jews. Rav Kook followed Rabbi Karo's ruling, and combined this view with the opinion we saw above, that shemitta today is rabbinic, concluding that the rabbinic level of sabbatical-year sanctity in modern times would be suspended by the sale of the land to a non-Jew.

The Ridbaz and others pointed out the paradox inherent in this position;[52] out of a commitment to the settling of the Land of Israel and a deep conviction of its sanctity, Rav Kook was willing to suspend that sanctity by selling it to non-Jews. Rav Kook responded to this challenge by distinguishing among various kinds and levels of holiness: "In situations where the biblical level of sanctity remains, the acquisition of land by a non-Jew does not suspend its sanctity; but when the level of sanctity is rabbinic, it is suspended by sale to a non-Jew."[53] He argued that there is a holiness to the Land of Israel and an intrinsic merit in living there that does not depend on the fulfillment of the commandments and therefore persists even if it is impossible, for whatever reason, to fulfill certain commandments:

> [The sages] said, "Settling in the Land of Israel is equal to all the other commandments of the Torah." This means that settling there in itself is the [manifestation of the] primary sanctity of the Land of Israel. The merit of the agricultural commandments relating to the land is drawn along with it as a result. Yet even when [the precepts relating to the land] are suspended because of an urgent situation, [the primary sanctity] remains intact.[54]

52. See section 15 of *Shabbat HaAretz*, "The Holiness of the Land of Israel and the Holiness of the Commandments," in this volume, for Rav Kook's response to the Ridbaz.
53. *Shabbat HaAretz*, 115.
54. Ibid., 118.

May One Sell the Land of Israel to Non-Jews?

The biblical prohibition of *lo teḥonem* (Deut. 7:1–2) was divided by the rabbis into three prohibitions[55] – one of them being interpreted to mean that you shall not give them (i.e., idolaters) a foothold in the land. This was widely understood as a prohibition against selling the land to non-Jews and was therefore an obstacle to the *heter mekhira.*

Rav Kook marshaled a number of arguments against this objection.[56] He cited the suggestion of his colleague on the Jaffa rabbinical court, Rabbi Zalman Shach, that the prohibition of giving "a foothold in the land" could only be transgressed by selling land to a non-Jew who did not already have "a foothold," that is to say, did not own land in Israel before the sale. This would leave just a rabbinic prohibition against selling land to non-Jews who already had land, since this changed the degree of their ownership but not the fact of ownership.

More fundamentally, Rav Kook argued that prohibiting the *heter mekhira* on the basis of *lo teḥonem* would be entirely self-defeating. Surely, the purpose of the law in Deuteronomy was to promote Jewish ownership of the Land of Israel, whereas literal observance of shemitta without the *heter* would cause Jews to leave their land and possibly return to Europe. Maintaining the underlying principle of the law required making an exception. Moreover, he asserted, one could rely on the opinion of the great medieval scholar Rabbi Menachem HaMeiri (1249–1315) that non-Jews who follow monotheistic religions are not to be considered idolaters. Meiri defined a new halakhic category, *umot hagedurot bedat,* nations that were bound by a religion and that therefore, unlike idolaters, subscribe to moral norms.[57] Meiri took Christians and Muslims of his day to fall into this category; consequently, they were exempt from restrictions that the halakha had applied to lawless idol worshipers.

---

55. Avoda Zara 20a.
56. See section 12 of *Shabbat HaAretz;* in this volume, see p. 103, "The prohibition of 'Give them no foothold…' in selling land to a non-Jew."
57. Meiri makes use of this concept in a number of places in his talmudic commentary, most extensively in *Beit HaBeḥira,* Avoda Zara, p. 46. For a penetrating exploration of Meiri's understanding of non-Jewish religions, see Moshe Halbertal's "Between Torah and Wisdom: Rabbi Menachem HaMeiri and the Maimonidean Halakhists in Provence" (Jerusalem, 2000).

For those unwilling to rely on Meiri, Rav Kook argued that one could employ the widely held opinion of Maimonides[58] that Muslims were not idolaters and that therefore the prohibition on selling land in Israel did not apply to them.[59]

Are Legal Fictions Justified?

Rav Kook was seriously exercised by the questions of whether legal fictions in general were justified in Jewish law and, if so, whether a fictitious sale was effective in a case where the clear intent of the parties was to evade a law and not to effect a lasting transfer of ownership. Rav Kook concluded that the use of legal fictions was, in certain circumstances, justified. "The Jerusalem Talmud states that to be merciful with the property of Israel, it is permissible to evade [the law]. And where there is great necessity, as seems to be the case regarding the question of the sabbatical laws, in view of the current situation, it is proper, according to this [principle], to rule leniently."[60] The long-standing practice[61] of selling leavened products to non-Jews for the duration of Passover to evade the prohibitions on a Jew seeing or owning such food during the holiday established a halakhic precedent for fictitious sales.

Rav Kook argued, ingeniously, that whereas in a normal commercial transaction both parties need to intend a full transfer of ownership, in a sale to evade a prohibition, it is enough that both parties intend

58. Maimonides, *Mishneh Torah, Hilkhot Avoda Zara* 10:6.
59. A halakhic prohibition on selling land or other property to non-Jews would significantly compromise the State of Israel as a country in which all citizens have equal rights. A group of rabbis publicly asserted such a prohibition in 2010, to widespread outrage. Many of the arguments deployed by the majority opposing the ban draw on reasons cited by Rav Kook to justify the *heter mekhira* sale, in particular, his argument that non-Jews living in Israel today are not idol worshipers. For a good English summary of the issues, see "Responsum: Attitude Toward Members of Other Nations Living in the State of Israel," eng.beithillel.org.il/responsa/attitude-toward-other-nations-living-in-state-israel/.
60. Y. Beitza 3:2; *Shabbat HaAretz*, 109.
61. As Rav Kook himself notes, this loophole started to be used widely in the early modern period when Jews became involved in brewing beer on a large scale and forcing brewery owners to destroy their stocks before Passover would have entailed ruinous financial loss.

a sale for this purpose alone.[62] Paradoxically, the very fictitiousness of the sale becomes an advantage. The crucial question for Rav Kook was, what are the values and meta-halakhic principles for the sake of which it is warranted to employ legal fictions?

Meta-Halakhic Principles of *Shabbat HaAretz*

Shabbat HaAretz became a defining piece of Religious Zionist *psak halakha* (halakhic decision making) and has served as a lightning rod for controversy between Religious Zionists and Ḥaredim about the proper parameters of halakhic innovation in Israel. It owes this status to Rav Kook's openness about the meta-halakhic principles that motivated and justified his embrace of the *heter*. These principles revolve around a recognition of the *national* dimensions of the return to Israel. Halakha in Israel, he believed, must strive to find solutions for the collective rather than being content to regulate the lives of observant individuals or subsectors.[63]

First, Rav Kook explicitly invoked the value of enabling Jews to live and flourish economically in the Land of Israel as a justification for the *heter*: "What would we say in a situation that affects the *nation as a whole* in reference to the settlement of the Jews in their land? Would not everyone certainly agree that it is permissible to rely on a lone opinion in matters that are rabbinic by nature?"[64]

Second, he asserted that the Land of Israel was the national center of the whole Jewish people. Believing that concerns about shemitta were deterring religious Jews from immigrating, he felt responsible to find a

62. "We must certainly say that in a transaction for the purpose of making a business deal, the primary intent is the fulfillment of the deal...but when the essence of the transaction is to suspend a prohibition, and both the seller and the buyer have the intent to sell and buy, this intent is enough.... For the fact that he buys it so it will be considered his for the purpose of suspending the laws of the sabbatical year, on this they definitely have intent and it is of benefit to the Jew to sell it and to the non-Jew to buy it" (*Shabbat HaAretz*, 111).

63. Arye Edrei, "From Orthodoxy to Religious Zionism: Rabbi Kook and the Sabbatical Year Polemic," trans. Shmuel Peerless, http://www2.tau.ac.il/InternetFiles/news/UserFiles//Shemitta.pdf (2008), 107–9.

64. *Mishpat Kohen* (Jerusalem: Mossad HaRav Kook, 1966), 63.

solution that would enable these Jews to move to the Land of Israel with confidence that shemitta observance would not destroy their livelihood.[65]

Third, as Arye Edrei convincingly shows, Rav Kook was concerned with expanding the target audience for his halakhic decisions from the religiously observant of the Old Yishuv to all Jews living in the Land of Israel, whether observant or not. When the Ridbaz suggested to Rav Kook that they solve the shemitta issue by going to Europe to raise money to support religious farmers who wished to cease work in the shemitta, Rav Kook responded that this was a solution for small numbers but not for the majority.[66] He felt responsible to make the halakha work – at least as a potential option – for the whole Yishuv, even those who currently identified as outsiders to the observant community.

THE INTRODUCTION TO *SHABBAT HAARETZ*: THE AGGADA OF SHEMITTA

Shabbat HaAretz is a rigorous and detailed halakhic treatment of what was and was not to be done in the shemitta of 1909–10 and why. Characteristically, Rav Kook prefaced the book with an introduction written in an entirely different register. These pages are a poetic and mystical paean to the possibilities of shemitta. Their principal point of connection to the halakhic work is in Rav Kook's argument, briefly discussed above, that the talmudic sages enjoined the continued observance of shemitta as a reminder of what it could one day be. The introduction is an ecstatic effort to render the reminder as vividly as possible.

In this prefatory section, Rav Kook paints a picture of shemitta as enabling a renewed connection to the divine life force in each individual and within us collectively. Like Sabbath, shemitta quiets the tumult of the intervening periods and restores a more authentic relationship to ourselves, to one another, to nature, and to God. Its observance reveals the unique weave of socioeconomic relationships that the Torah would have us pattern. The Jubilee year is a revelation of the cumulative insight and holiness that we will have achieved in the previous seven shemitta cycles. Its ideals of liberty and emancipation bear universal meanings

65. Ibid.

66. Edrei, "From Orthodoxy to Religious Zionism," 100.

for the whole of humanity. Rav Kook outlines a biblically based schema of Jewish history in which our ancestors' avaricious neglect of shemitta led to exile from the Land of Israel and a prolonged divorce from the earthly, physical dimensions of life. This lengthy period of ethereal existence refined the people's ethical sensibility, and they began once more to long for a return to their homeland. Rav Kook hoped that this nascent resettlement of the land would lead one day to the mitzvot connected to the land, shemitta foremost among them, being observed in all their glory. Yet he realized that the state of the agricultural pioneers was still precarious and that most would need to avail themselves of the *heter mekhira*, so that the Yishuv could continue to grow and flourish to the point where full shemitta observance would eventually be possible. Meanwhile, he urged his readers to continue to study all they could about shemitta, as learning led to action and would help bring closer the day when shemitta would be observed in Israel as it should be.

But how *should* it ideally be observed? Clearly, Rav Kook hoped that one day it would be possible for all the halakhot of shemitta to be operational, including observance of the prohibitions against doing most forms of agricultural labor. But he envisioned much more: a periodic outbreak of justice, equality, psychic rebirth, and restored universal human dignity amounting to a comprehensive spiritual and social renewal. How does Rav Kook help us to understand what that would look like or how to go about getting there?

Although Rav Kook's prose in the introduction is lyrical and rather short on specifics, there are a number of places where he provides us with striking images of what the ideal shemitta or Jubilee might be like. These can provide highly suggestive and stimulating guideposts. Some of them point along lines that contemporary thinkers and activists are already pursuing; others are arrestingly original. I will briefly discuss seven of them.

1. Shemitta is for the community what Sabbath is for the individual.

"What Sabbath does for the individual, shemitta does for the nation as a whole," writes Rav Kook in the introduction. "Just as it was said about the Sabbath of Creation, 'It is a Sabbath for God,' so, too, it was said about the Sabbath of shemitta: 'It is a Sabbath for God.'" Shemitta, like Sabbath, is envisaged as a time for us all to step out of the nonstop scramble of getting and spending and to renew ourselves, restoring our connection with the unique, divine life that flows in each one of us. What might this mean today? Daniel Taub, who from 2011 to 2015 served as Israel's ambassador to the U.K., beautifully expressed the possibilities of a universal sabbatical in an essay that he wrote:

> [Shemitta is a] time to see ourselves not in terms of what we do, but what we are, and even what we might become.... For any of us, to learn that instrument, to write that book, to try the path we never took.... The cost – decommissioning a seventh of the productive workforce – might sound steep. But it is an investment with potentially exponential rewards. For the workplace: a continuous stream of invigorated employees, brimming with insights and experiences; for families: a time for reacquaintance and renewal; for society: an opportunity for caring individuals to devote not just the margins of their weeks but the very kernels of their days to the underprivileged; for culture: an invitation to untapped masses to learn to appreciate, to explore, and to create; for our youth: a promise that passion and opportunity will not be buried forever with their first paycheck; and, perhaps most of all, for our seniors: a chance to prepare for the increasingly traumatic transition to retirement and to preempt the dread "if only" that threatens to haunt our final years.[67]

2. Shemitta is an expression of the interconnection between people and land.

Rav Kook views shemitta as an outstanding instance of the inextricable connection between the people and the Land of Israel. Both embody an innate rhythm that longs for and requires relief and renewal once every seven years. As Rav Kook puts it in the introduction to *Shabbat HaAretz*:

> The distinctive character of the people and the land dovetail with each other. Just as the people has a special aptitude for reaching

67. Daniel Taub, "Scratching the Seven-Year Itch" (unpublished essay, 2000).

> spiritual heights from within the depths of everyday life, so, too, the land – God's land – forms the people who dwell there as an everlasting inheritance that comes through a covenant and promise, with faith in the Eternal One of Israel, and is founded on the divine nature immovably infused in this wonderful country, which is married to the people whom God chose. The soul of the people and the land intertwine, working from the basis of their being to bring into existence the intricate patterns of inner holiness that lie within them during the sabbatical year. The people works with its soul force on the land, and the land works on the people, refining their character in line with the divine desire for life inherent in their makeup.

The people and the land both need a year of Sabbath!

Rav Kook's sensibility and meaning in speaking of the connection between people and land were closer, I would suggest, to those of the great American prophet of agrarianism, Wendell Berry, than to Gush Emunim.[68] The land for Rav Kook was not primarily important as an abstraction. He wrote and, apparently, thought little about land as a political category. He was patently thrilled by participating in the Jewish people's reacquaintance with the earthy facts of its ancestral homeland. Whether kissing stones, crying as he placed a sapling tree into the soil, or gleefully traveling in a dirty hay cart when he visited the settlement of Merhavia, Rav Kook rejoiced in the reality of knowing, seeing, and touching the particular places that had been formative of the Jewish people's spiritual character. His enthusiasm for the pioneering farmers and laments about the impoverished character of a Diaspora Judaism that had been exiled from the soil are reminiscent of Wendell Berry's complaints about a Christianity that had become cut off from physical, biological reality; or, as Berry put it: "My own long held belief that Christianity, as usually presented by its organizations,

68. Gush Emunim was the movement established in 1974 to settle the territories of Judea and Samaria, also known as the West Bank. Founded by students of Rav Kook's son, Zvi Yehuda, the faithfulness or otherwise of the settlement movement to the spirit of Rav Kook's teachings has been much debated.

is not *earthly* enough – that valid spiritual life, in this world, must have a practice and a practicality – it must have a material result."[69] (Or, as he puts it more pithily, "I don't think it is appreciated how much of an outdoor book the Bible is.")[70]

A consciousness of the interwovenness of the Land of Israel with the Jewish people and its history, culture, and religion pervades the introduction to *Shabbat HaAretz*. It should not, I would contend, be read through the prism of political developments that occurred long after Rav Kook's death; rather, it is a call to recover the awareness that Berry writes of when he says:

> We have given up the understanding – dropped it out of our language and so out of our thought – that we and our country create one another, depend on one another, are literally part of one another; that our land passes in and out of our bodies just as our bodies pass in and out of our land; that as we and our land are part of one another, so all who are living as neighbors here, human and plant and animal, are part of one another, and so cannot possibly flourish alone; that, therefore, our culture must be our response to our place, our culture and our place are images of each other and inseparable from each other, and so neither can be better than the other.[71]

3. In the shemitta year, treat food as food, not as a commodity.

> Claims to private property will not profane the holiness of the produce of the land during this year, and the urge to get rich, which is stimulated by trade, will be forgotten; as it says, "for you to eat – but not for your trade."

69. Wendell Berry, "The Gift of Good Land," in *The Gift of Good Land: Further Essays Cultural and Agricultural* (Berkeley: Counterpoint, 1981), 267.
70. Wendell Berry, *The Art of the Commonplace: The Agrarian Essays* (New York: Counterpoint, 2003).
71. Wendell Berry, *The Unsettling of America* (San Francisco: Sierra Club, 1977).

Rav Kook emphasizes the principle, rooted in a number of halakhot of shemitta, that in that year, food is for eating, not for trading. The biblical verse says, "The sabbatical produce shall be for you *to eat*" (Lev. 25:6), based on which uses of the produce, other than directly eating it, are restricted. As Maimonides codified it in his *Mishneh Torah*: "We may not use the produce of the sabbatical year for commercial activity. If one desires to sell a small amount of the produce of the sabbatical year, he may.... He should use it only to purchase food and eat that food according to the restrictions of the holiness of the sabbatical year."[72] In the sabbatical year, produce grown in Israel becomes sanctified. Its holiness is honored when we eat it as food but desecrated if we use it for profit through trading the food as a commodity.

The global food business today is worth trillions of dollars, and it is treated as an industry like any other. The industrialization of agriculture has enabled the mass production of cheap food that has fed millions, especially in the Third World, but has also come with serious costs. This shemitta principle challenges us to return to a more natural and immediate relationship to the food we eat – for example, by eating more *food* rather than food-like products manufactured from dozens of artificially synthesized ingredients.[73]

4. Shemitta is a year of human health.

> Human beings will return to a state of natural health, so that they will not need healing for sicknesses, which mostly befall us when the balance of life is destroyed and our lives are distanced from the rhythms of nature; "for you to eat" but not to make medicine and not to use as bandages.

Rav Kook here makes the astonishing claim that in the shemitta, people will naturally return to a state of physical health. He bases this on the halakha that in the shemitta, food products should not be used to make

72. Maimonides, *Mishneh Torah, Hilkhot Shemitta VeYovel* 6:1.
73. Michael Pollan makes this provocative distinction in *In Defense of Food* (New York: Penguin, 2008).

bandages, poultices, and other medicinal products. This is also based on Lev. 25:6, which teaches that you should view the produce of shemitta "as food" – but not, the rabbis infer, as medicine.[74] Rav Kook suggests that such things simply will not be necessary in the ideal shemitta; health will flow from a restoration of natural equilibrium.

Only the most extreme natural-health fanatic would take such a claim at face value, rather than as hyperbole or messianic dreaming. Conversely, only the narrowest adherents of a mechanistic, biomedical approach to health and illness could fail to be struck by Rav Kook's insight that lifestyle imbalance tends to cause disease (or dis-ease, as holistic health practitioners prefer to write it). Decades before the development of the medical research field of psycho-neuro-immunology, which demonstrated that prolonged stress suppresses the immune system and is a causative factor in a spectrum of diseases ranging from heart disease to depression, Rav Kook points out that ceaseless activity is bad for us and that the rest and renewal that shemitta offers can promote health and healing.

5. Shemitta and the Jubilee are interconnected rhythms and structures.

> Holiness grows throughout these spans of time: "Count the shemitta years in order to sanctify the Jubilees,"[75] to prepare life for the Jubilee. "And you shall count off seven weeks of seven years – seven times seven years – so that the period of seven weeks of seven years gives you a total of forty-nine years."[76]

Insight and consciousness build over each shemitta cycle, until a kind of culmination at the end of seven cycles, with the Jubilee and an outbreak of universal freedom and emancipation. Rav Kook sees the Jubilee and shemitta cycles as intimately connected. This chimes with Rav Kook's embrace of R. Yehuda HaNasi's halakhic position (outlined above)

74. Sukka 40b, Mishna Shevi'it 8:1.
75. Arakhin 32b.
76. Lev. 25:8.

that since Jubilee and shemitta are interdependent and the Jubilee is not operative in our times, shemitta today is only a rabbinic obligation.

Shemitta observance is cumulative. Rav Kook emphasized that this cumulative characteristic of shemitta results from our moral choices to deepen and broaden the implementation of the values and practices of shemitta. He believed that whereas the impulse and need to observe shemitta is innate, the potential of shemitta to grow and evolve with each round of observance depends on how we choose to practice it. The implication of this insight is that renewed interest in shemitta and experimentation around its public forms should grow and deepen, cycle by cycle. Through each iteration, our understanding of the possibilities of shemitta may grow into new structures of observance and consciousness that we cannot currently imagine.

6. Jubilee is a year of truth and reconciliation.

> The spirit of the Jubilee will gather great strength, until it has sufficient potency not only to reveal the goodness within the soul of the people, … as does the shemitta, but also to fix the crookedness and brokenness of the past…. "Then you shall sound the horn loud; in the seventh month on the tenth day of the month – the Day of Atonement – you shall have the horn sounded throughout your land,"[77] and a godly spirit of general forgiveness, such as the individual experiences on Yom Kippur, will arise through the holiness of the Jubilee…. From Rosh HaShana until Yom Kippur, slaves would neither become free to go home, nor would they remain slaves to their masters, but they would eat, drink, and rejoice with crowns on their heads. When Yom Kippur would arrive, the *beit din* would sound the shofar, slaves would be free to go home, and fields would return to their original owners.[78]

The Jubilee was a time when slaves went free and land returned to its ancestral owners. Whatever inequalities had accumulated in the previ-

77. Lev. 25:9.
78. Rosh HaShana 8b.

ous forty-nine years, the Jubilee restored each to his original dignity. Rav Kook gives a beautiful reading of a talmudic passage that fills in the interpersonal dimension of this economic drama. The Talmud points out a contradiction between the Mishna (Rosh HaShana 1:1), which says that the first day of Tishrei – Rosh HaShana – is the start of the Jubilee, and the verse in Leviticus 25 that says that the shofar blast marking the start of the Jubilee and the freeing of slaves was sounded on the tenth of Tishrei – Yom Kippur. When did the Jubilee start, and when were slaves actually freed? By way of resolution, the Talmud quotes the opinion that slaves were freed from servitude on Rosh HaShana but only free to go home after the shofar blast on Yom Kippur. In the interim, they ate, drank, and celebrated with their former masters.

By quoting this in the context of the view of the Jubilee as a year of forgiveness that "rectifies the injustices of the past," Rav Kook frames the scene of the slaves feasting on an equal footing with their erstwhile owners during their final days together as integral to that process of forgiveness. The Torah also requires the master to send off his servants with gifts. These leveling acts help heal the social scars and psychological wounds caused by economic divisions and class estrangement. Rav Kook recognizes that national healing requires not just freeing the slaves; the indignity and humiliation that they endured over many years must also be addressed and overcome. One wonders whether he foresaw the failures of revolutionary movements that treated economic emancipation as a sufficient goal and ended up merely switching out the ruling class while perpetuating oppression and cruelty.

7. Jubilee is a universal principle.

> Such life-affirming flights of possibility [in the Jubilee year] will raise up the people to bind its life together with all humanity through those special people, the *gerim toshavim* – non-Jews who… feel a special connection to the reinvigorated spiritual aspirations of the Jewish people…. "The law of a Hebrew servant and the law of the *ger toshav* operate only when the Jubilee operates."[79]

79. Arakhin 29a.

Rav Kook intuited that there is a strong universal dimension to the idea of the Jubilee. He inferred this from the talmudic statement that the institution of *ger toshav* is only operational in an era when the Jubilee is in force. *Ger toshav* is a status for non-Jews who feel drawn to the Jewish people and take upon themselves to observe the seven Noahide laws in the Land of Israel. Rav Kook understood there to be an inner connection between the two concepts; the *gerim toshavim* would be the channel through which the ideals of the Jubilee reach all humanity.

Neither the laws of Jubilee nor of *ger toshav* operate today, and it is unclear whether or how either will ever be reinstated. Nevertheless, Rav Kook's sense of the universal appeal of the Jubilee ideal was clearly correct. Other Jewish thinkers have also seen in the Jubilee economic thought that could apply beyond the boundaries of the Jewish people. Rabbi Samson Raphael Hirsch advocated the Jubilee as a universal antidote to economic inequality in his Bible commentary; in 1930, the Revisionist Zionist thinker Ze'ev Jabotinsky wrote an important essay arguing that the biblical Jubilee idea should be the blueprint for the future economic system because it avoided both the suffocating control of socialism and the obscene inequalities of unbridled capitalism.[80]

Early American thinkers repeatedly invoked the Jubilee to express the universality of freedom. In 1751, when the Pennsylvania Assembly ordered a special bell to be cast, commemorating the fiftieth anniversary of William Penn's Charter of Privileges, the Speaker of the Assembly was entrusted with finding an appropriate inscription to express the charter's aspirations to freedom and equality. What later became the Liberty Bell inscription was taken from the biblical verse describing the Jubilee year: "Proclaim Liberty thro' all the Land to all the Inhabitants thereof" (Lev. 25:10). The Jubilee idea inspired the United States Homestead Act of 1862, which parceled out land holdings to small farmers. The influential nineteenth-century American economist Henry George took the Jubilee idea as the inspiration for the theory that there should be a single tax on land to prevent land speculation, which George saw as the main

80. Samson Raphael Hirsch, *The Hirsch Chumash* (New York: Feldheim, 2009), and Ze'ev Jabotinsky, "The Jubilee Ideal," in Jabotinsky, *Nation and Society* (Tel Aviv: Beitar, 1961), 62–67.

cause of entrenched economic inequality. (The game of Monopoly was invented by a follower of George as an educational tool to demonstrate the evil effects of rent in impoverishing tenants and enriching landlords.)

More recently, the Jubilee 2000 movement took the Jubilee as the inspiration for its demand that $90 billion of Third World loans be forgiven so as to lift the crippling effects of historical debt and give dozens of developing countries a new chance to grow and flourish. In the aftermath of the 2007–9 crash, in which debt and economic inequality were both centrally implicated, Jubilee thinking resurfaced once again. It is safe to assume that the Jubilee concept has not exhausted its potential as a universal source of inspiration for radical economic reform.

CONCLUSION: THE TEXT

Rav Kook's introduction to *Shabbat HaAretz* is a difficult and opaque text. It combines lyrical poetry, kabbalistic speculation, sweeping (though often also profound) schematizations of Jewish history, reflections on the socioeconomic possibilities of shemitta, and a justification for the halakhic work that follows. As in most of his writings, here, too, Rav Kook quotes biblical, talmudic, and kabbalistic sources, mostly without attribution. Sometimes he rereads these sources in brilliant and insightful ways, creatively recasting them as resources for his argument.

The introduction panoramically scans Jewish history 2,500 years into the past, but its vision primarily focuses on the future. Rav Kook gazes forward to a fuller and richer realization of shemitta than was possible in the precarious economic circumstances of his time and place. His vision is suffused with passionate longing and sometimes reality merges into the messianic horizon. Yet within it, we can discern contours of a future that, with the benefit of being a century closer to it than Rav Kook, we might also recognize as possible.

Note on the Translation

Translating Rav Kook's writings is a challenging privilege. The privilege lies in the immense profundity, beauty, and importance of his writings; it is a joy to make them more widely available to the English-speaking world. Among the challenges: his sentences are often very long; the syntax can be confusing; the style and vocabulary are influenced by a genre of nineteenth-century belles lettres that is long out of fashion; the subject matter is frequently esoteric or mystical; he quotes from the whole repertoire of traditional Jewish sources, usually without attribution; and occasionally, the thought that he is expressing remains elusive even after repeated rereading of a sentence or passage.

In his classic essay on English style, "Politics and the English Language," George Orwell gives six rules for writing. Number six is "break any of these rules sooner than say anything outright barbarous." I have strained to convey Rav Kook's meaning while staying as close as possible to his syntax, sentence structure, and word choice. Occasionally, however, I saw no alternative but to break the rules in order to render Rav Kook's thought in non-barbarous English.

שבת הארץ / הקדמה

מאת הרב ר׳ אברהם יצחק הכהן קוק זצ״ל

ראשי פרקים על ערך השמיטה והיובל בחיי ישראל בכלל
ובתחית האומה, הארץ והתורה, באור ד׳, חי העולמים

Introduction to *Shabbat HaAretz*

Rabbi Abraham Isaac Kook

A summary of the value of shemitta and yovel in the life of the Jewish people generally and in the revival of the nation, the land, and the Torah, in the light of God, Life of the World.

הקדמה

ומי כעמך כישראל גוי אחד בארץ (שמואל ב', ז', כ"ג).

גוי אחד בארץ, ודאי בארץ הם גוי אחד, עמה אקרון אחד ולא אינון בלחודייהו (זהר ויקרא צ"ג, ב').

השמיטה והיובל בזמנים, מתיחסים זה לזה, כמו החמה והלבנה בעולם וכמו ישראל והאדם בנפשות – יחס הפרט והכלל, שהם, במובנם העצמי היותר חי ויותר רוחני, צריכים זה לזה: פרט הצריך לכלל וכלל הצריך לפרט.

---

1. In choosing this quotation from the Zohar, the classic work of Jewish mysticism, as the epigram for his book about shemitta, Rav Kook suggests that the uniqueness of the Jewish people is fully manifested only when they are living on their land and practicing the laws that regulate life in harmony with the earth – shemitta foremost among them.
2. In Leviticus 25, the primary biblical source for shemitta, the sabbatical and Jubilee years are interconnected parts of a fifty-year cycle; see Lev. 25:2–10.
3. Rav Kook alludes here to the foundational kabbalistic notion of *ashan*, an acronym of *olam, shana, nefesh*, or world, time, and soul, the three dimensions that shape the finite world. The concept of *ashan* first appears in *Sefer Yetzira*, the oldest extant work of Jewish mysticism, references to which occur in texts from the first century

Introduction

> Who is like Your people Israel, a unique nation on earth? (II Sam. 7:23)

> "Who is like your people Israel, a unique nation on earth?" When they are united with the land, they are called a unique nation, but not when they are separate from it. (Zohar, Leviticus 93b)[1]

The sabbatical and Jubilee years are interconnected in time,[2] like the sun and the moon in the universe, like Israel and humanity in the world of souls.[3] The particular and the universal are profoundly interdependent in the most vital and spiritual sense; the particular needs the universal, and the universal needs the particular.[4]

(see *Sefer Yetzirah*, trans. Aryeh Kaplan [York Beach, ME: Samuel Weiser, 1990], 4:7–4:14). Rav Kook's otherwise rather enigmatic reference to the sun and moon as instances of the particular and the universal appears to refer back to *Sefer Yetzira* 4:7. See *Orot HaKodesh* (Jerusalem: Mossad HaRav Kook, 1938, 1985), 2:313, for an expanded explanation of Rav Kook's understanding of the holiness inherent in these three basic dimensions of existence.

4. The interdependence of the particular and the universal is a major theme in Rav Kook's writings. For an especially penetrating discussion of the relationship between these poles of Rav Kook's thought, see Yehudah Mirsky, *Rav Kook: Mystic in a Time of Revolution* (New Haven, CT: Yale University Press, 2014), 107–11. See also the introduction to this volume.

"מי גוי גדול אשר לו אלהים קרובים אליו!" – סגולתה של כנסת ישראל היא, שהיא מסתכלת על ההויה כולה באספקלריא המאירה של קודש. בכל עוז חייה היא מכרת, שהחיים שווים הם את ערכם רק באותה מידה שהם אלהיים, וחיים שאינם אלהיים אינם שווים לה מאומה. היא יודעת עוד, שבאמת אין חיים אלא אלהיים, וחיים שאינם אלהיים אינם חיים כלל, והידיעה הזאת, המונחת בעומק תכונת נשמתה, מטבעת עליה את חותם ערכה המיוחד לה, המוטבע על כל יחיד ויחיד מיחידיה. כי אורו וישעו של היחיד תלויים הם במידת ידיעתו את התעמקותו והתלבטותו של החותם הזה, של הכרת ערך החיים רק באלהיותם, בתוך נשמתו. "ואתם הדבקים בה' אלהיכם, חיים כולכם היום".

החיים, על פי ערך האלהיות שבהם, אינם מתגלים אל היחיד אלא באותה מידה, שהוא מתאמץ להיות נשאף בכל הוויתו בתוכיותה של כללות האומה, להיות מוזהר מזוהר נשמתה העליונה, החיה וקיימת בהכרת היקר האלהי של החיים מתוך פנימיותה הכללית.

טבע הנשמה הכללית של כנסת ישראל הוא אלהיותה. לא בחירתה גרמה לה את יתרונה האלהי, לא מצד מעשיה הפרטיים, לא בצדקתה ויושר לבבה באה אל מעלתה: תכונת גזעה, הגופני והרוחני, עשתה לה את חילה ואת עוזה באלהים, אשר לא בבחירה לקחה אותו ולא תוכל כל קלקלה של בחירה לאבדו. יש לה, אמנם, להבחירה מבוא גדול בכל סגולה טבעית, בהיותה טובה תוכל לפנקה, לעדנה, להוציאה לפועל באופן שלם וחשוב, וכן בהיותה רעה ושפלה

5. Deut. 4:7. Note that elsewhere, Rav Kook cites this biblical passage explicitly in the context of elaborating the goal of creating an exemplary and enlightened socioeconomic order in Israel. E.g., "In order to fulfill this aspiration, it is particularly necessary that this community possess a political and social state and national sovereignty at the peak of human culture – 'surely a wise and understanding people is this great nation'" (Deut. 4:6) (*Orot* [Jerusalem: Mossad HaRav Kook, 1993], 104).

6. Holiness is a central concept in Rav Kook's thought. For an insightful discussion, see Norman Lamm, "Harmonism, Novelty and the Sacred," in *Rabbi Abraham Isaac Kook and Jewish Spirituality*, ed. Lawrence J. Kaplan and David Schatz (New York: New York University Press, 1995), 159–77; see also the introduction to this volume.

7. Deut. 4:4.

8. Rav Kook uses the word *neshama* here for "soul." This is the highest of the three levels of soul that are commonly discussed by the kabbalists: *nefesh*, *ruaḥ*, and *neshama*. See the introduction to this volume.

"For what great nation is there that has a God so close at hand?"[5] What is remarkable about the Jewish people is its ability to view existence through the lens of holiness;[6] it knows, with the full force of its being, that life has the greatest value to the extent that it is infused by godliness and that a life without a touch of the divine is not worth anything. Even more than that, they know that a godly life is true life, and life without God is no life at all. This knowledge, lying deep within the people's soul, gives it a unique character and impresses itself on each and every one of her individual members. The light and salvation of each person depends on the depth and force of this imprinting awareness that the value of life is in its godliness. "And you, who held fast to the Lord your God, are all alive today."[7]

Life in its fullest, divine intensity is increasingly revealed to a person to the extent that he struggles to aspire with all his being to connect to the inner life of the people as a whole and to be illuminated by the light of its exalted spirit; the spirit lives through a pervasive inner awareness of the precious godliness in life.

The essential quality of the Jewish people's collective soul is its divine nature.[8] The people did not gain this characteristic[9] through its choices, actions, righteousness, or good character. It is a core quality, both physical and spiritual, that gives the people divine force and strength. It was not acquired through choice, and no choices can negate it. Choices, however, can powerfully affect the state of this innate quality.[10] The people can decide to nurture, develop, and perfect it; alternatively,

9. The nature of the Jewish people's difference from other nations is a classic issue in Jewish thought; the key medieval protagonists were Yehuda Halevi and Maimonides. See introduction to this volume for further discussion of Rav Kook's relation to their views.

10. Rav Kook expresses here in brief his view that the holiness of Israel depends on two main elements: an innate *segula,* or soul force; and the choices to do good or bad that each of us makes. He believed that the *segula* force was the greater and that it would grow stronger still in the period of the "footsteps of the Messiah." See *Iggerot HaRe'aya* 2:186–88 (Jerusalem: Mossad HaRav Kook, 2002) for an expanded discussion of this. For a good English summary, see Michael Z. Nehorai, "Halakhah, Metahalakhah, and the Redemption of Israel: Reflections on the Rabbinic Rulings of Rav Kook," in *Rabbi Abraham Isaac Kook and Jewish Spirituality,* ed. Kaplan and Schatz, 122–24.

תוכל להחשיך את המאור שבסגולה הטבעית ולעכר את זהרו, לטמטם את הלב לבל יחוש את העושר הרוחני הצפון בתוך חיי הנשמה. אבל לא יוכלו טמטום הלב והחשכת המאור להימשך לעולם. הסגולה הטבעית בטוחה היא בקיומה ובהתעוררותה לתחייה.

סגולת האומה – הטוב האלהי הטבוע בקרבה, סדר העולם, החיים הישרים והטובים המתאימים אל הצדק והיושר, השקט והשלווה, החן והאומץ הממולאים בהסתכלות אלהית מקפת, כפי מה שהיא נמצאת בנשמת האומה – אין חיי החול יכולים להוציאה מן הכוח אל הפועל. חיים אלה במהומתם המעשית התכופה מסתירים הם את ההוד הרוחני של הנשמה האלהית, ומעכבים את הזרחת אורה הבהיר והישר לתוך המציאות החילונית השולטת. דחיפת הגידול וההשתלמות של החיים צריכה שתצא אל הפועל על ידי נתינת רוח, של הפסקה והתנערות, ממהומת החיים הרגילה.

היחיד מתנער מחיי החול לפרקים קרובים – בכל שבת. "בא שבת באה מנוחה", מתחלת הנפש להשתחרר מכבליה הקשים, "ביום הניח ד' לך מעצבך ומרגזך ומן העבודה הקשה אשר עובד בך", ומבקשת היא לה אז נתיבות עליונות, חפצים רוחניים, כפי טבע מקורה, "טוב להודות לה' ולזמר לשמך עליון, להגיד בבקר חסדך ואמונתך בלילות, עלי עשור ועלי נבל, עלי הגיון בכנור". "ביני ובין בני ישראל אות היא לעולם!" יום קדוש, אשר בו תתגלה נטיית האומה – הנטייה של החיים האלהיים כמו שהם – ביחידיה אות היא לאומה, שיש בסגולת נשמתה צורך ויכולת להתענג על ה' – ונועם אלהי, המתכנס לנקודה רוחנית של נשמה יתרה, שרוי בלבו של כל יחיד מבניה.

---

11. The inevitability of spiritual renewal is a theme of Rav Kook's book on repentance, *Orot HaTeshuva* (Jerusalem, 1994). See, e.g., ch. 1, where repentance is described as a natural health-restoring impulse; 4:2, where the repentance of the individual is an expression of a movement toward *teshuva* active in the whole universe; and 15:10, where the individual's *teshuva* is presented as a return to authentic selfhood.
12. Rashi on Gen. 2:2. Rashi's full comment reads: "What was lacking [in Creation]? Rest. Enter Sabbath, enter rest; and then the work of Creation was finished." Creation was not complete until rest was made to complement and balance creative activity.
13. Isa. 14:3.
14. Ps. 92:1–4. This is the "Psalm for the Sabbath Day."
15. Ex. 31:17.

bad choices will darken its light, muddy its glow, and stupefy hearts so that they will no longer sense the spiritual riches hidden in the life of the soul. But darkness and stupefaction cannot continue indefinitely. Sooner or later, this inner soul treasure can be relied upon to arouse the nation to renewal.[11]

This national treasure that is imprinted deep within us, the image of a world that is good, upright, and godly – aligned with peace, justice, grace, and courage, all filled with a pervasive divine perspective that rests in the spirit of the people – cannot be actualized within a way of life that is purely secular. Such a life, full of frenetic action, veils the glory of our divine soul, and the soul's clear light is blocked from shining through the overpowering, mundane reality. The impulse toward growth and self-realization needs space to come to fruition. We need to stop and shake off the bedlam of our daily lives.

The individual shakes off mundane routine frequently – every week. "Shabbat comes and so does rest!"[12] The soul begins to shed her harsh chains. "The Lord has given you rest from your sorrow and trouble and from the hard service that you were made to serve."[13] The soul then seeks higher pathways of spiritual desire that are consonant with the nature of her source. "It is good to praise the Lord, to sing hymns to Your name, O Most High, to proclaim Your steadfast love at daybreak, Your faithfulness each night with a ten-stringed harp with voice and lyre together."[14] "It shall be a sign for all time between Me and the people of Israel."[15] This is a holy day when the innate inclination of the people for a godly life emerges from its hiddenness and is a sign for the people that its soul treasure contains within it the need and the ability to rejoice in God, in the delight of the divine. This is concentrated in the point of the extra soul[16] that dwells within each one of the people's children.

16. Rav Kook refers to the "extra soul" that, according to tradition, Jews possess on the Sabbath. The talmudic source is Beitza 16a, which interprets the words *shavat vayinafash* (Ex. 31:17) as *Vay (avda) nefesh!* ("Alas for the soul that is lost!" – at the end of Sabbath). Interpretations of this idea have ranged from the more rational, e.g., Ibn Ezra and Radak, who argue that the soul that "is given rest on this day from the affairs of the world can occupy itself with wisdom and the words of God" (commentary to Gen. 2:3), to the more mystical, e.g., Nahmanides, who takes issue with Ibn Ezra and writes that "although his view of this is right to those who believe

את אותה הפעולה, שהשבת פועלת על כל יחיד, פועלת היא השמיטה על האומה בכללה. צורך מיוחד הוא לאומה זו, שהיצירה האלהית נטועה בקרבה באופן בולט ונצחי, כי מזמן לזמן יתגלה בתוכה המאור האלהי שלה בכל מלוא זהרו, אשר לא ישביתוהו חיי החברה של חול עם העמל והדאגה, הזעף והתחרות אשר להם, למען תוכל להתגלות בקרבה פנימה טהרת נשמתה בכללותה כמו שהיא. ואם אותה האביריות, המוכרחת להתלוות עם כל סדר של חיי ציבור קבועים, גורמת להקטין את עדינות החיים המוסרית, והניגוד המתמיד שבין השמיעה האידיאלית להכרזה של חסד ואמת, חמלה ורחמים, לבין הנגישה והכפייה ולחץ הקפדה של קניין ורכוש, המוכרחים להיראות בעולם המעשי, גורם הרחקה לאור האלהי מתכונת הכרתה הציבורית של האומה, שהרחקה זו מפעפעת כארס גם במוסרם של היחידים – הנה הפסקת הסדר החברתי בצדדים ידועים, מתקופה לתקופה, מביאה לאומה זו, כשהיא מסודרת, על מכונה, לידי עלייתה העצמית למרומי התכונות הפנימיות שבחיים המוסריים והרוחניים, מצד התוכן האלהי שבהם, העומד למעלה למעלה מכל תכסיס וסדר חברתי והוא מעבד ומעלה את הסדרים החברתיים ונותן להם את שלמותם.

"וכשם שנאמר בשבת בראשית, 'שבת לד'', כך נאמר בשביעית: 'שבת לד''". סגולת הארץ וסגולת האומה מתאימות יחד. כשם שהאומה היא מיוחדת להרוממות האלהית במעמקי חייה, כך הארץ, ארץ ד', היא מכשירה את העם היושב עליה בנחלת עולמים, הבאה בברית ובשבועה בביטחון נצח ישראל, המיוסד על הטבע האלהי הקבוע במטבע ארץ חמדה נפלאה זו, המזווגת לעם זה

in it, for this is not something that can be tested by experience… nonetheless you must understand that on the Sabbath, there is in truth an additional soul." (See also Zohar II 204a–b.) Rav Kook draws on elements of both schools here in understanding the "extra soul" as something that is always within us that we are able to access on Sabbath when the rush of weekday activity is stilled.

17. There is a note of suspicion about commerce in this passage. For a discussion of Rav Kook's relationship to socialist thought, see Shalom Rosenberg, "Introduction

What Sabbath does for the individual, shemitta does for the nation as a whole. The Jewish people, in whom the godly, creative force is planted eternally and distinctively, has a special need to periodically reveal the divine light within itself with full intensity. Our mundane lives, with their toil, anxiety, anger, and competition, do not entirely suffocate this creative force. During shemitta, our pure, inner spirit may be revealed as it truly is. The forcefulness that is inevitably part of our regular, public lives lessens our moral refinement. There is always a tension between the ideal of listening to the voice inside us that calls us to be kind, truthful, and merciful, and the conflict, compulsion, and pressure to be unyielding that surround buying, selling, and acquiring things.[17] These aspects of the world of action distance us from the divine light and prevent its being discerned in the public life of the nation. This distancing also permeates the morality of individuals like poison. Stilling the social order from time to time in certain predictable ways is meant to move this nation, when it is well ordered, to rise toward an encounter with the heights of its other, inner moral and spiritual life.[18] They touch the divine qualities inside them that transcend all the stratagems of the social order and that cultivate and elevate our social arrangements, bringing them toward perfection.

"Just as it was said about the Sabbath of creation, 'it is a Sabbath for God,' so, too, it was said about the Sabbath of shemitta, 'it is a Sabbath for God.'"[19] The distinctive character of the people and the land dovetail with each other. Just as the people has a special aptitude for reaching spiritual heights from within the depths of everyday life, so, too, the land – God's land – forms the people who dwell there as an everlasting inheritance that comes through a covenant and promise, with faith in the Eternal One of Israel, and is founded on the divine nature immovably infused in this wonderful country, which is married to the

to the Thought of Rav Kook," in *The World of Rav Kook's Thought*, ed. Benjamin Ish-Shalom and Shalom Rosenberg (Jerusalem: Avi Chai, 1991), 59–61. See also the introduction to this volume.

18. Cf. Rav Kook's idea of "the continuous prayer of the soul": the soul is always praying (i.e., yearning to unite with God). When we consciously pray, we rise to an encounter with the soul that is praying constantly (*Olat HaRe'aya* 1:1).

19. Rashi's commentary on Lev. 25:2.

אשר בחר לו יה לסגולתו. נשמת האומה והארץ יחדיו פועלות את יסוד הוויתן, תובעות את תפקידן, להוציא אל הפועל את עריגת קדושתן, בשנת שבתון. העם פועל בכוחו הנפשי על הארץ, זרע ד׳ מתגלה על ידי השפעתו הרוחנית, והארץ פועלת על העם, להכשיר את תכונתו לפי חפץ חיים אלהיים שלמים בתבניתם.

שנת שבתון מוכרחת היא לאומה ולארץ!

שנת שקט ושלווה, באין נוגש ורודה, ״לא יגוש את רעהו ואת אחיו כי קרא שמיטה לה׳״, שנת שוויון ומרגוע, התפשטות הנשמה בהרחבתה אל הישר האלהי המכלכל חיים בחסד, אין רכוש פרטי מסוים ולא זכות קפדנית, ושלום אלהי שורר על כל אשר נשמה באפו. ״והיתה שבת הארץ לכם לאכלה, לך ולעבדך ולאמתך ולשכירך ולתושבך הגרים עמך, ולבהמתך ולחיה אשר בארצך תהיה כל תבואתה לאכל״. אין חילול קודש של קפדנות רכוש פרטי בכל תוצאות יבולה של שנה זו, וחמדת העושר, המתגרה על ידי המסחר, משתכחת – ״לאכלה ולא לסחורה״. עין טובה והוקרה נאמנה באה לכל, ברכת ד׳ אשר בפרי הארץ, ״לאכלה ולא להפסד״. והאדם חוזר אל טבעו הרענן, עד אשר לא יצטרך לרפואות למחלות, שהן באות ברובן על ידי הריסת המשקל של החיים, בהתרחקם מטהרת הטבע הרוחני והחמרי ״לאכלה, ולא למלוגמא ולא לרפואה, ולא לעשות ממנה אפיקטוזין״. רוח קדושה ואצילות שפוך על פני כל, ״שנת שבתון יהיה לארץ – שבת לה׳!״.

20. Deut. 15:2. The verse quoted refers to the remission of debts in the shemitta and prohibits creditors from exacting payment from debtors.

21. Lev. 25:5–7.

22. Mishna Shevi'it 7:3. In this passage, Rav Kook draws on a series of halakhic midrashim based on a phrase from Lev. 25:6, "for you to eat," which is interpreted to exclude making use of food grown in the Land of Israel during the shemitta for purposes other than eating.

people whom God chose. The soul of the people and the land intertwine, working from the basis of their being to bring into existence the intricate patterns of inner holiness that lie within them during the sabbatical year. The people works with its soul force on the land, and the divine seed is revealed through its spiritual influence; the land, too, works on the people, refining their character in line with the divine desire for life inherent in their makeup.

The people and the land both need a year of Sabbath!

A year of peace and quiet, where there are no tyrants or taskmasters; "he shall not oppress his fellow or kinsman, for the remission proclaimed is of the Lord";[20] a year of equality and relaxation in which the soul may expand toward the uprightness of God, who sustains all life with loving-kindness; a year when there is no private property and no standing on one's rights, and a godly peace will pervade all that breathes. "It shall be a year of complete rest for the land, but you may eat whatever the land will produce during its Sabbath – you, your male and female slaves, the hired and bound laborers who live with you, and your cattle and the beasts on your land may eat all its yield."[21] Pernickety claims to private property will not profane the holiness of the produce of the land during this year, and the urge to get rich, which is stimulated by trade, will be forgotten; as it says, "for you to eat – but not for your trade."[22] A spirit of generosity will rest on all; God will bless the fruit of the land "for you to eat and not your loss." Human beings will return to a state of natural health, so that they will not need healing for sicknesses, which mostly befall us when the balance of life is destroyed and our lives are distanced from the rhythms of nature; "for you to eat" but not to make medicine and not to use as bandages.[23] A holy spirit will be poured out upon all life; "it will be a year of complete rest for the land – a Sabbath of the Lord."[24]

---

23. Sukka 40a. See the introduction to this volume for further discussion of Rav Kook's astonishing claim that shemitta will promote a natural state of human health that will make medicine unnecessary.
24. Lev. 25:4–5.

בשנה זו מתגלה צביונה של האומה בכליל הודה, במקור רוחה האלהי. והארה זו, הבאה אחת לשבע שנים, מושכת אחריה עליות אידיאליות אלהיות, שבהכשרן האטי של הנשמות הן הולכות וכובשות להן מקום בחיים, עד שהשקפות החיים הנובעות ממנה נעשות יותר ויותר קבועות ומסוימות ופועלות, עד בוא תקופה יותר ארוכה, יותר חשובה, שהיא מספקת כבר להעלות לא רק את אישי האומה היחידים ולא רק את כללותה בדור ההווה היחידי כי אם את הדורות שלה. היובל, זוהי תקופה הרת עולם, הערוכה מיסוד החופש האלהי העליון.

סדר החיים של שנת השמיטה הוא על פי החפץ הפנימי הטבעי של תשוקת הטוב והצדק, השוויון והמנוחה, שההכרה האלהית ותשוקתה מטביעה בקרב האומה, אשר אין זה לזה תכונה חיקויית, דבר מלומד מן החוץ, כי אם נחלתה הטבעית, ממקורה עצמה. אבל מקור ישראל כשמתגלה בטהרו איננו עומד על עמדו, מתגבר הוא תמיד ומתרחב והולך. מקנה הוא לעצמו את אומץ הפעולה וכוח ההשפעה וסופג לתוכו את העילוי של הבחירה הטובה, התשובה הטהורה, המתגברת בתגבורת האלהיות של החיים כפי מקור ישראל. נמשך הוא והולך בקדושתו בכל משך הזמן של הפרקים, "מונין שמיטין לקדש יובלין", להכשיר אליו את החיים. "וספרת לך שבע שבתות שנים שבע שנים שבע פעמים, והיו לך ימי שבע שבתות השנים תשע וארבעים שנה". ומצינור החיים של היובל, שהוא הולך במעלות שלביו ומתפשט עד בואו אל חיי האומה בצביונם הפרטי, יונקת היא השמיטה ומתמלאת את זיווה השלם והרענן, המתגלה בה מתשוקתה אל הסדר האלהי שיחול במלוא כל היקום ולא רק בקרבה פנימה, לבדה.

והולך ומתעלה הוא הרוח, עד שנצבר כוח גדול ועצום, שיש בו די אונים לא רק לגלות את הטוב שישנו במזומן באוצר חיי האומה, לשמור את צביון החיים, כמידתה של השמיטה, כי אם גם לישר את המעקשים והקלקולים של העבר ולהעמיד את מצב חיי האומה על פי הוויתה המקורית, להשיבם לימי

25. As does the Sabbath.

26. As does the shemitta.

In this year, the divine character within the people will be revealed in its glory. This once-every-seven-year illumination carries an afterglow of divine ideals that will gradually shape our ethical characters so that the outlook that flows from them will become a deeper and more formative part of us, until a longer, significant period has elapsed – enough to raise up not merely individuals[25] or just the collective in a particular generation,[26] but all the generations that lived during that period. The Jubilee is a time of rebirth for the whole world, grounded in divine freedom.

Life during the shemitta year is guided by the natural, inner desire for goodness and justice, equality, and calm, which God has planted within the nation. The people did not become like this by imitating something external; it is part of its nature. When this inner life starts to reveal itself in all its purity, it does not stand still. It is expansive and generous, seeking the power to act and to influence its surroundings. Israel's inner nature soaks up the elevating power of its good choices, which restore our lives and the pure penitence that reconnects us to the source of the Jewish people's inner strength. Holiness grows throughout these spans of time: "Count the shemitta years in order to sanctify the Jubilees,"[27] to prepare life for the Jubilee. "And you shall count off seven weeks of seven years – seven times seven years – so that the period of seven weeks of seven years gives you a total of forty-nine years."[28] Shemitta will suckle from the life channels of the Jubilee, which will gradually rise and spread, until they give shape to the life of the people. From those sources will the shemitta be filled with a wholesome and invigorating glow that will arise out of the yearning for a divine order that fills all existence and not merely its own inner being.

The spirit of the Jubilee will gather great strength, until it has sufficient potency not only to reveal the goodness within the soul of the people and protect its form of life, as does the shemitta, but also to fix the crookedness and brokenness of the past and to reestablish the

27. Arakhin 32b. The Talmud describes here how the advent of the Jubilee was to be calculated.

28. Lev. 25:8.

העלומים ברעננות מטעה, ולגלות לא רק מה שגנוז בטבעה של נשמת האומה בפועל כי אם מה שמוכשר להיגלות ולהאיר בקרבה, על ידי עזרת התגלות הטבה הבחירית שלה, שהיא צריכה להעיר את ההתרוממות היובלית.

האומה נותנת אות, שהכשירה את עצמה בימי התגלות סגולתה הטבעית אל העליוניות הרוממה הזאת, שכישרונה יוכל להגיע לה בהכרה הנשגבה של אלהיות החיים, וההכרה מתעוררת, שיש רוח חדשה המבשרת צבא רב, "והעברת שופר תרועה בחדש השביעי בעשור לחדש ביום הכפורים תעבירו שופר בכל ארצכם" רוח אל עליון של הסליחה הכללית, הפוגשת את כל יחיד בכל יום הכיפורים, מתעלה כאן בקדושת היובל לצביון כללי, בהתלבש האומה ברוח סליחה ותשובה לישר את כל עיוותי העבר. "וקראתם דרור בארץ לכל יושביה", "מראש השנה עד יום הכיפורים לא היו עבדים נפטרים לבתיהם ולא משתעבדים לאדוניהם. אלא אוכלין ושותין ושמחין ועטרותיהן בראשיהן. כיוון שהגיע יום הכיפורים תקעו בית דין בשופר, נפטרו עבדים לבתיהן ושדות חוזרות לבעליהן" (ראש השנה ח׳ ב׳). אין הדרור הזה פורץ כהר פרצים, כי נמשך והולך הוא מן הקודש העליון, איננו יוצא בתור יוצא דופן מתוך המעגל החברתי המסודר, כי מתוכו ומעצמותו הוא נובע, מתוך סדר החיים של התקופות הקצרות הקדומות, עד הגיעו לידי מידתו זו, שהוא מתחיל להתרומם בפעולת כישרונה של האומה בהתגלותה הבחירית, בתיקון העיוותים של העבר.

אם ירדו יחידים מהאומה ממדרגת החיים המלאים אור קדוש וחופש, וייעשו לעבדים בשכחם את ערכם האצילי, ו"און ששמעה על הר סיני: 'כי לי בני ישראל עבדים, עבדי הם ולא עבדים לעבדים' – והלך זה וקנה אדון לעצמו", הנה באה השבת הכבוד האישי וחירותו, מתוך זרם חיים של קדושת עליון

29. Ibid. 25:9.

30. Ibid. 25:10.

31. Rosh HaShana 8b. See the introduction to this volume for a discussion of Rav Kook's original reading of this talmudic passage.

32. Lev. 25:55.

33. Kiddushin 22b. The Talmud here censures the Hebrew slave referred to in Ex. 21:6, who elects to remain a slave beyond the mandatory period. His choice shows that he

people's existence on its original pattern. It can restore a pristine freshness to our lives, not only through what is already present, albeit hidden in our souls, but also through what is being prepared to reveal itself and illuminate us by the power of our free choice to do what is good – which must awaken in the exalted Jubilee year.

In these years, when its inner character is being revealed, the nation gives a sign that it is preparing itself for an even higher level; one that can lead to a keen awareness of the godliness in life. The awakening of such awareness heralds a new spirit that announces great things: "Then you shall sound the horn loud; in the seventh month on the tenth day of the month – the Day of Atonement – you shall have the horn sounded throughout your land,"[29] and a godly spirit of general forgiveness, such as the individual experiences on Yom Kippur, will arise through the holiness of the Jubilee and spread throughout the entire society, clothing the whole people in a spirit of repentance and acquittal that will straighten out the injustices of the preceding period: "You shall proclaim release throughout the land for all its inhabitants."[30] From Rosh HaShana until Yom Kippur, slaves would neither become free to go home, nor would they remain slaves to their masters, but they would eat, drink, and rejoice with crowns on their heads. When Yom Kippur would arrive, the *beit din* would sound the shofar, slaves would be free to go home, and fields would return to their original owners.[31] This freedom does not erupt like some volcano; it emerges gradually from the higher holiness. It is not a radical exception to the regular social order but flows from within it, nurtured by the life of the shorter, preceding periods until, reinforced by the revelation of our choices for good, it has the power to repair past injustices.

If individuals fall from the status of free men and women and, forgetting their inherent nobility, are made into servants – "the ear that heard the words at Sinai, 'the children of Israel are My servants,'[32] *My servants, and not the servants of My servants,*" and yet in spite of this he

---

has not internalized the innate freedom and dignity that attaches to being a servant of God, not of man. Rav Kook understands the return of each person to his ancestral land as the remedy for the indignity of selling oneself as a slave.

השופע מהמקור היותר עליון, שממנו האומה יונקת את אור נשמתה – ודרור נקרא בארץ לכל יושביה. ולעומת אי־שוויון המשקל של מצב הרכוש הקרקעי, שהוא בא מרפיון ידיים ורוח מכל חטאות האדם, המכשילות את כוחו, עד שהוא יורד מנחלת אבותיו, באה השבה, המתאמת כפי ערכה של האומה בראשית מטעה, ברכוש היסודי הזה לאותם אשר הכבידה עליהם תגרת החיים ותעוות את משקלם, "בשנת היובל הזאת תשובו איש אל אחוזתו".

ודווקא בתעופה מלאה חיים כמו אלה מתרוממת האומה לרכוס את חייה עם חיי האדם בכללו, על ידי אמצעותם של אישים יחידים – הגרים התושבים – העומדים בכללותם בתוך האנושיות הכללית ומרגישים בקרבם גם כן יחס מיוחד אל נטיותיה הרעננות ושאיפותיה הרוחניות של האומה, ודווקא אז מתכנסת בה התקיפות הפנימית לדחוק את החלק הסיגי שבעצמה, כדי שיאיר יפה המאור הכללי המבהיק. "אין עבד עברי נוהג ולא גר תושב נוהג אלא בזמן שהיובל נוהג" (ערכין כ"ט א').

כל אלה יחד הם סימני חיים עליונים, שצריכה לגלותם אומה זו, שמוסר לאומי אלהי כזה חי בקרבה, ונכון הוא לפניה, בהיותה מבונה בכל תכסיסיה ברום עילויה המדיני "כשכל יושביה עליה" – למען יעלה בידה תכסיס התגלות ההכרה של היושר האלהי, העומד למעלה מסגולתה המוכנה עמה מכבר, השומרת על תפקידיה שלא ירדו ולא יימחו כליל.

כשהבחירה המקולקלת משקעת את אור עילוי החיים של "רחובות הנהר", ההולך ומשתפך גם מעל לגבול ישראל, היא פוגמת את יסוד הסגולה

34. Lev. 25:10.
35. Ibid. 25:13.
36. Arakhin 29a. See the introduction to this volume for a short discussion of how Rav Kook reads this talmudic passage and the universal aspects of the Jubilee.
37. Arakhin 32b. The Talmud sets "when all its inhabitants are living there" as a condition for the observance of the Jubilee year. This is inferred from the verse referring to the Jubilee, "freedom is proclaimed throughout the land to *all its inhabitants*" (Lev. 25:10), i.e., the Jubilee's proclamation of freedom may occur only when all the land's inhabitants are living on it. Rav Kook understands that the fulfillment of this condition effects a qualitative change in the people's political situation.

went and acquired a human master for himself[33] – now his freedom and self-respect are returned to him. Holiness flows into our lives from the highest source, the place from which the nation's soul suckles light and "freedom is proclaimed throughout the land to all its inhabitants."[34] Inequality in landed property, which resulted from bodily and spiritual weakness and error, sapped his strength, until he was forced to sell his ancestral patrimony. Now, however, restitution comes, corresponding to the people's status at the beginning of its journey. The original property returns to those who have suffered from the vicissitudes of life, distorting their sense of their true value: "In this Jubilee, everyone shall return to his original holdings."[35]

Such life-affirming flights of possibility will raise the people up to bind its life together with that of all humanity through those special people, the *gerim toshavim* – non-Jews who stand fully in the mainstream of universal humanity and who also feel a special connection to the reinvigorated spiritual aspirations of the Jewish people; then there will arise an inner urge in the people to rein in the separatist element within itself so as to properly highlight the brilliant illumination of the universal: "The law of a Hebrew servant and the law of the *ger toshav* operate only when the Jubilee operates."[36]

All these are signs of a spiritual vitality that this people will manifest when a divine sense of morality is alive within them. They will emerge from the complexity of the nation's political situation in its full richness, "when all its inhabitants are living there."[37] Thus will the people find a way to reveal an awareness of the godly integrity that stands above its innate quality, that is already within it, and that protects the people's purposes so that they do not decline or disappear entirely.

When corrupted choice darkens the light of the life of "broad spaces by the river,"[38] which grows and overspills the borders of Israel,

---

38. Hebrew, *reḥovot hanahar*: a kabbalistic term based on Gen. 36:37, meaning the broadening of wisdom. Rabbi Schneur Zalman of Liadi, the founder of Chabad, characterizes *reḥovot hanahar* as the spreading of the kabbalistic *sefira* of *ḥokhma* (wisdom), which he likens to a wellspring, into the *sefira* of *bina* (intellect), which he compares to a river (*Likutei Torah, Shir HaShirim* 39b).

הטבעית. אי־אפשר לה אמנם להכחידה, אבל בידה להשקיעה במעמקים, עמוק־עמוק, עד אשר תיעלם זמן רב, עידן ועידנים, והעם יקו לאור ואין, עד בוא עת קץ.

התורה, בדעותיה, חוקיה ומשפטיה, לחיי היחיד והציבור, היא האספקלריא המאירה, שבתוכה משתקפת כל מעלת רוח האומה, בין הרוח הסגולי הטבעי של השמיטה ובין רוח עליון רוח אלהים חיים של היובל, המתגלה בהתגלותה הבחירית. כל זמן שהיא משתמרת, ברוחה ובפעליה, בתוך האומה והארץ וסדרי החברה, הרי היא נותנת עוז ותעצומות לעם. הדבקות באלהים הרעננה משעשעת היא אז את נשמת החיים שלו ומרננת את הלב של כל פרט. היא הולכת וזורמת על אור האמונה האלהית על פי הכרתה של האומה מצד נשמת סגולתה הטבעית, אשר בירוריה התולדתיים שהיא מעוטרת בהם, בנורי ישועה מדור דורים, הם מכשירים את הכרתה האלהית המיוחדת לפי צביונה הפרטי. וההכרה המיוחדת הזו הולכת ופועלת וחוזרת ומתפעלת מהטוב הכללי של אור אלהים, שבאדם ובעולם, היא מטיבה אותו, מסגלת אותו אליה בהטביעה בו את צביונה הפרטי, ומכשירתו בזה למלא חדרי כל רוח ונפש ברגשי טוהר וחדוות יושר המבוססים בנצחיותם בעדנם האלהי, שהוא מצילם מכל ייאוש ומשגבם ישע עדי עד.

עולה היא האומה ברום מעלותיה אלה – כשהיא מכרת את רוחה העצמי. הכרה זו היא מביאה אותה להיעטר בגודל לבב בתורת אלהים אשר עימדה, היא מרכיבתה על במתי ארץ. ועד כמה שיהיו חיי כל הסביבה כולה בלתי־מוכשרים או מנוגדים לאותה הרוממות האלהית, שרוח ישראל שואף אליה, לא תילכד במצודתם, ואת דרכה תלך לבטח. אז תעורר את סגולת טבעה ואת הוד חיל בחירתה אחריה. השמיטה והיובל יחדיו יהיו תמים על ראשה והארץ תענה לעומתה בחילה הרוחני האצור בקרבה, המתאים לחדוות השמיטה

such choice mars the foundation of Israel's natural excellence – though it cannot destroy it. But it can plunge that treasure deep, deep down into the depths, until it disappears for a long time, eons and eons. The people will long for light, when there is none, until the time of the End.

The Torah, with its ideas, statutes, and laws, for the life of the individual and the community, is a clear glass, in which all the spiritual qualities of the people are reflected – whether the natural, intrinsic impulses that are expressed in observance of shemitta, or the higher, divine spirit of the Jubilee, which is manifested through the people's choices. So long as the Torah is observed, both in letter and in spirit, in the people, the land, and in the way society is ordered, it gives strength to the nation. The reenergizing closeness to God will then thrill the life soul of the people and bring joy to the heart of each individual. The light of faith will stream through the consciousness of the people from its natural, distinctive spirit; the refinements of this spirit that take place generation by generation will adorn the people, dedicated, as they are, to salvation from time immemorial, and these refinements will train the people's unique, divine consciousness according to its individual character. This distinctive awareness will continually do its work, and will in turn be worked upon by the universal good of divine light. This light sharpens our awareness and stamps upon it its particular form, enabling it to fill up all the recesses of spirit and soul with pure feelings and upright joy, which are founded eternally on divine delight, which saves one from all despair and raises up everlasting salvation.[39]

The people rises to these levels when it knows its own particular spirit. This self-knowledge allows the people to be crowned with the divine Torah that stands at the summit of the world. However inhospitable, or even hostile, the surroundings are to the godly heights for which Israel yearns, she will not be caught in their snares but will go confidently on her way. Then her natural inner character and the splendor of her power of moral choice will be awakened. The shemitta and the Jubilee will adorn her, and the land will respond to the people, with all the

39. The second half of this paragraph is especially unclear.

ורננת היובל. ״וצויתי את ברכתי לכם בשנה הששית ועשת את התבואה לשלש השנים״. ״ירעפו נאות מדבר וגיל גבעות תחגרנה״. ״לבשו כרים הצאן ועמקים יעטפו בר, יתרעעו אף ישירו״.

כשעוממה בישראל הכרת הרוח העצמי ״זנח ישראל טוב״, שכח את עוזו וגאוותו. המבט החיצוני על הסביבה הרחבה הבלתי־מפותחת, הפראית בטבעה ובבחירתה גם יחד, השכיח ממנו את גדולת סגולתו. אז הוסעו מן הלב תשוקת החיים האלהיים ועדניהם וחמדת משושם וחילם בהתגלמם בפועל, בארץ החיים. טהרת השכל הפשוט והברור הושבתה, זיו הצדק הועם. את עמדתם לקחו הדמיון הגס של החברה הפרועה ורשע כסל של ההזיות האליליות ותועבותיהן. במשאון כוסתה הסגולה האלהית האצולה בנשמת האומה ולא תוכל עוד לקחת לב חמדת חיי טוהר, שקט ויושר. תכונת האומה ברדתה הוסיפה ירידה גם לתכונת רוח הארץ, שהוא מתאים עמה התאמה ניצחת. בחולשת נשמת האומה לא תיתן סגולת הארץ את תפקידה. רוח הארץ, רוח ארץ חמדה המלאה שירת קודש ורננת־יה, ירד מטה־מטה. ״ותטמא הארץ ואפקד עונה עליה, ותקיא הארץ את יושביה״. רוח האומה בכללה ספג אל תוכו יסודות רעים וזרים, עד אשר העיב את טהרתו העצמית. ״כי זנתה אמם, הובישה הורתם״. אף בכל הציורים היותר קדושים, החתומים באפיה של האומה, הוטל הרעל, ״חדשיכם ומועדיכם שנאה נפשי, היו עלי לטרח, נלאיתי נשא״. והחיים הלאומיים, אחרי אשר הוטמאו, הוסיפו לה חיילים מוסריים כבירים, ויהיו עם שאונם המדיני רק למהומה פנימית המהממת את הנפש. שני היסודות, האומה והארץ, אשר בבריאותם הם מוסיפים זה לזה כל כך לווית חן, כל כך אומץ ועוז,

40. Lev. 25:21. The verse promises God's blessing on the sixth year so that the shemitta will not cause shortage or hardship.
41. Ps. 65:13–14. The antecedent of "it," in the previous verse (65:12), is "God's bounty." Rav Kook cites this verse as an image of blessing and plenty.
42. Hos. 8:3. See also *Orot HaKodesh* 3:140, where Rav Kook cites the same biblical verse to connote the spurning – by the individual or community – of one's unique, divine source of being.

spiritual goodness that is within her, attuned to the joy of shemitta and the Jubilee. "I will ordain My blessing for you in the sixth year so that it shall yield a crop sufficient for three years."[40] "The pasturelands distill it; the hills are girded with joy. The meadows are clothed with flocks, the valleys mantled with grain; they raise a shout, they break into song."[41]

When Israel's awareness of its own spirit became foggy – "Israel rejects what is good"[42] – the people forgot its strength and pride. Looking superficially at their undeveloped and wild environment made them forget their inner greatness. The yearning for a refined, godly life slipped from their hearts, as did the sense of joyful strength that one has when life is clothed in deeds. Clear, simple, pure-hearted understanding ceased, and the light of justice was dimmed. In its place came the coarse imagination of a lawless society, and the dumb, evil delusions of idolatry, with all its attendant abominations. Under their burden, the sublime, divine character of the people was smothered, and there were no more pure, upright, and serene hearts. This moral collapse in the nation was matched by a decline in the spiritual character of the land, which had always been intertwined with the moral life of the people. As the people became spiritually weaker, the special qualities of the land could no longer find fulfillment. The spirit of the precious land, full of holy song and godly gladness, plummeted. "Thus the land became defiled; and I called it to account for its iniquity, and the land spewed out its inhabitants."[43] The people absorbed bad influences, which coarsened its pure nature. "In that their mother has played the harlot, she that conceived them has acted shamelessly."[44] Even the most holy images engraved on the face of the people became toxic: "Your new moons and fixed seasons fill Me with loathing. They have become a burden to Me, and I cannot endure them."[45] When national life became defiled and also suffered intense moral sicknesses, with the surrounding political turmoil, the result was simply inner anguish and confusion. These two elements – the people

43. Lev. 18:25.
44. Hos. 2:7. The prophet compares Israel's pursuit of idolatry to an adulterous woman's pursuit of lovers.
45. Isa. 1:14. In this passage, God rejects the people's ritual worship when their moral life is full of oppression and cruelty.

החלו משפיעים זה לזה בחלותם – לרעה ולזוועה, עד אשר הוכרחה לקחת מעמד הרפואה הרחמנית האכזרייה, הניתוח הנורא, התרחקות האומה מהארץ "ומפני חטאינו גלינו מארצנו ונתרחקנו מעל אדמתנו".

בעצם צרתה הגדולה של האומה, כאשר סר מקרבה שאונם של החיים הלאומיים ומהומתם המזקת, החל האור הרוחני לשוב לעלות לאטו בקרבה במעלות אשר ירד. רוח האומה הוסיף להעלות אבר כפי מידת שביתתו מהחיים המדיניים, שהם ראשונים לטומאה בציבור מקולקל.

ואמר אליה: ימים רבים תשבי לי, לא תזני ולא תהיי לאיש, וגם אני – אליך. כי ימים רבים ישבו בני ישראל אין מלך ואין שר, ואין זבח ואין מצבה ואין אפוד ותרפים (הושע ג׳, ג׳-ד׳).

והיה ביום ההוא, נאם ה׳, והכרתי סוסיך מקרבך והאבדתי מרכבתיך, והכרתי ערי ארצך והרסתי כל מבצריך. והכרתי כשפים מידך ומעוננים לא יהיו לך, והכרתי פסיליך ומצבותיך מקרבך ולא תשתחוה עוד למעשה ידיך (מיכה ה׳, ט׳-י״ב).

והשמתי אני את הארץ, ושממו עליה אויביכם הישבים בה. ואתכם אזרה בגוים, והריקתי אחריכם חרב, והיתה ארצכם שממה ועריכם יהיו חרבה. אז תרצה הארץ את שבתתיה כל ימי השמה ואתם בארץ איביכם, אז תשבת הארץ והרצת את שבתתיה. כל ימי השמה תשבת את אשר לא שבתה בשבתתיכם בשבתכם עליה.

46. Taken from the *musaf* prayer for the new moon and festivals.

47. Hos. 3:3–4. In this passage, the betrayed husband takes back his previously unfaithful wife, giving her merely "fifteen pieces of silver, a homer of barley, and a *letekh* of barley." Similarly, God resumes His intimacy with the Jewish people but removes from them the trappings of national sovereignty, which had aided their betrayal.

48. Mic. 5:9–12.

49. Lev. 26:32–35. These verses imply that exile was the punishment for not observing

and the land, which, when healthy, had given each other so much grace and power for good – made each other sicker and more corrupt. Finally, they had to take the cruel-kind medicine, the dreadful surgical operation of separating the people from the land – "Because of our sins, we were exiled from our country and distanced from our land."[46]

From deep within the people's terrible troubles, after their turbulent national life with all its destructive turmoil had been taken away from them, their spiritual light and strength began gradually to return to the levels from which it had declined. The people's spirit began to soar again, the longer they were separated from politics and statecraft – which are poisonous to a broken society.

> I stipulated with her: in return, you will go a long time without either fornicating or marrying; even I shall not cohabit with you. For the Israelites shall go a long time without king and without officials, without sacrifice and without cult pillars and without ephod and teraphim.[47]

> In that day, I will destroy the horses in your midst and wreck your chariots. I will destroy the cities of your land and demolish all your fortresses. I will destroy the sorcery you practice, and you shall have no more soothsayers. I will destroy your idols and the sacred pillars in your midst; and no more shall you bow down to the work of your hands.[48]

> I will make the land desolate, so that your enemies who settle in it shall be appalled by it. And you, I will scatter among the nations, and I will unsheathe the sword against you. Your land shall become a desolation and your cities a ruin. Then shall the land make up for its Sabbath years, throughout the time that it is desolate and you are in the land of your enemies; then shall the land rest and make up for its Sabbath years. Throughout the time

---

shemitta; during the years of dispersion, the land will make up for the sabbaticals that were not properly kept while the Jewish people dwelled in the land.

והארץ תעזב מהם ותרץ את שבתתיה, בהשמה מהם והם ירצו את עונם, יען וביען במשפטי מאסו ואת חקתי געלה נפשם (ויקרא כ"ו, ל"ב-ל"ה).

ישראל בגולה עזב את דאגתו מכל ענייני חול מצד כללות האומה. שם את עיניו ולבו רק בשמים ממעל. לבו לא הלך עוד להרבות חיל, רכב וסוס, ככל גוי על אדמתו, ובכלל לא היה עוד לכלל האומה שום עסק חומרי. יחד עם זה חדל לעגב אל כל תזנוני הגויים הרבים. ורוח ה' החל לפעמו להשכיל על ערך האדם ומעלת נשמתו, וכן להוקיר בייחוד את ערכה הרוחני של האומה ויתרונה האלהי. התורה נתחבבה עליו מזהב ומפז רב כבימי נעוריו הטובים. על קדושת האמונה והמצוות יצא להורג בשמחת לבב. עיניו ולבו, אשר היו בשמים תמיד, העלו ארוכה לכל משובות החיים הלאומיים ולכל פשעיהם), ומעת אשר התרחק מארצו פנה תמיד אליה, אבל לא במבט גס, לא ככל שוכן בית חומר המשתוקק אל ארץ מכורתו מפני שהיא משביעתו לחם ומספקת לו את חפציו החומריים, כי בעיניים מלאות חיבת קודש הביט אליה, אל סגולתה הפנימית, המתאימה לתשוקה האלהית אשר החלה לשוב לתוכו.

כן הארץ התנערה מטומאתה. "שִׁכּורי אפרים", שרים סוררים וחברי גנבים, אוהבי שוחד ורודפי שלמונים, הבועטים מרוב טובה, נמחו ממנה יחד עם כל חוסנה ותפארתה.

אחר ימים רבים החלה, אמנם למשוך אליה לאטה נדחים יחידים – אבל רק בכוחה לאלהים, בקדושתה העליונה המתעלה על כל חפץ חיי חומר ודרישת משטרי לאום.

50. Lev. 26:43.

51. Ps. 19:11.

52. See Jer. 8:22.

53. Isa. 28:1. The full verse reads: "Ah, the proud crowns of the drunkards of Ephraim, whose glorious beauty is but wilted flowers on the heads of men bloated with rich food, who are overcome with wine."

54. Rav Kook refers to the trickle of pious individual Jews who found their way to the Land of Israel from the thirteenth century onward. In the early nineteenth century, the numbers of such immigrants increased, motivated by the messianic expectations directed to the six-hundredth year of the sixth millennium (1840), based on prophecies of the Zohar. Between 1808 and 1840, the Jewish community in the Land of Israel more than doubled in size. The most notable group consisted of more than five hundred disciples of the Gaon of Vilna, who arrived around 1813. See Arie

> that it is desolate, it shall observe the rest that it did not observe in your Sabbath years while you were dwelling upon it.[49]

> For the land shall be forsaken of them, making up for its Sabbath years by being desolate of them, while they atone for their iniquity; for the abundant reason that they rejected My rules and spurned My laws.[50]

In exile, Israel abandoned its preoccupation with secular matters that concerned the people as a whole, and turned its eyes and hearts toward heaven. It stopped trying to amass power, chariots, and horses like every other people on earth, and the nation as a collective ceased all materialist pursuits. It no longer desired the debaucheries of the surrounding peoples. The spirit of God began to beat within the people once again and to awaken them to know the true heights of the human soul. So, too, they became aware once more of the Jewish people's spiritual potential. The Torah became more precious to them "than gold, than much fine gold,"[51] as it had been in the good times of the people's youth. They were willing to accept death joyfully for the sake of their holy faith and commandments. Their eyes and hearts, which were habitually cast heavenward, began to recuperate[52] from the backslidings and sins of their national life. From the time they were separated from the land, they turned toward it – not with the greedy gaze of one who sits in his house and desires to reacquire the land that he had sold because it supplied him with bread and other physical needs, but rather with a look of holy love for its inner character, befitting the godly desire that had begun to return to the people.

So the land will shake off the impurity of the "drunkards of Ephraim"[53] – the rebellious rulers and gangs of thieves who love bribery and pursue only their own gain, kicking against God out of their abundance of good things. They will melt away, along with all their power and glory.

Morgenstern, *Hastening Redemption: Messianism and the Resettlement of the Land of Israel* (Oxford: Oxford University Press, 2006), for an account of the fascinating and little-known episode of pre-Zionist Jewish immigration to Israel.

"קץ ישועה נסתם חרך". "לבא לפומא לא גליא". מי בא בסוד ד' לדעת מתי היטהרו כליל הארץ והגוי מטומאת הנידה אשר להם, מתי שב הרוח, המסתתר בעצמותו ונגלה בפעולותיו, כפי מידת הכשרת המצבים החיצונים המכשירים את התגלותו באומה ובארץ, אל טהרו וחוסנו, ומתי הגיעה עת דודים, אשר בהתחבר האומה והארץ יחד יפעל כל אחד מהם על חברו לטובה ולברכה, ולא כאשר היו בימי החשך, אין אתנו יודע עד מה. ובכן עינינו נשואות לחזות את חביוני המסתרים במקום רואים – בחזון קץ המגולה, אשר חכמים מאז הביעו: אין לך קץ מגולה מזה, שנאמר: "ואתם הרי ישראל, ענפכם תתנו ופריכם תשאו לעמי ישראל כי קרבו לבא". "ופניתי אליכם ונעבדתם ונזרעתם, והרביתי עליכם אדם כל בית ישראל כולה, ונושבו הערים והחרבות תבנינה, והרביתי עליכם אדם ובהמה ורבו ופרו והושבתי אתכם כקדמותיכם והטיבתי מראשתיכם, וידעתם כי אני ד'".

כל עוד שלא כלה זעם, כל זמן שבמעמקי רוח האומה והארץ לא סרה עדיין חלאתם מהם, היתה אז כל סיבת פנותם רק אל על, אל קדוש ד', רק מרוב שוממותם, מפני שלא היה להם כל עניין לקחת לב אדם החי חיי חומר עלי אדמות. אבל אם יתגלו אז בחיי חברה ומשטר ארץ, מיד יתגלה רוח העוועים אשר בחובם וההשחתות העתיקות תשובנה ותקיצינה. בכן נסתם עד אז כל חזון רוח, הארץ נשכחה כמת מלב כלל האומה, והיחידים שעלה על לבם לפנות אליה, לא היה להם כלל שום עניין המתייחס לצדה החומרי הארצי.

55. This appears to be a reference to Rashi's comment on Gen. 49:1: Jacob "wished to reveal the messianic end, but the divine presence was removed from him." See also Rashi's source, Genesis Rabba 98:2.

56. Ecclesiastes Rabba 12:10.

After a long time, scattered individuals gradually began returning to the land, drawn there by God's hand and by the holiness of the land rather than by any concern with material well-being or with reestablishing national government.[54]

"The appointed time of salvation is concealed."[55] "What is in the heart is not revealed to the mouth."[56] Who can know God's secrets and say precisely when the impurity of the land and the people will be lifted, when the spirit, hidden in its essence but revealed in its actions, will return once again in response to improvements in the outward situation that enable its reappearance in strength and purity upon the people and the land? When will the time of lovers come again, when the people and the land will reunite and mutual goodness and blessing will flow from their relationship – not like in the days of darkness? No one knows. So we raise our eyes to see the signs that are hidden in plain sight. In their vision of the messianic era, the sages said that "there is no messianic portent more obvious than this:"[57] "But you, O mountains of Israel, shall yield your produce and bear your fruit for My people Israel, for their return is near. For I will care for you: I will turn to you, and you shall be tilled and sown. I will settle a large population on you, the whole house of Israel; the towns shall be resettled and the ruined sites rebuilt. I will multiply men and beasts upon you, and they shall increase and be fertile, and I will resettle you as you were formerly, and will make you more prosperous than you were at first. And you shall know that I am the Lord."[58]

So long as the anger has not been assuaged, and so long as the sickness in the depths of the people's soul has not been fully cured, there was every reason for them to turn only to heaven for support. Because of the extent of the land's destruction, people were not interested in trying to live a life closely tied to the earth; if dreams of restoring political sovereignty had occurred to them then, their confusions and ancient

57. Sanhedrin 98a. See also Rashi ad loc. "When the Land of Israel generously gives of her fruits, then redemption is drawing near; there is no more obvious sign of the messianic end than this." Rav Kook urges paying attention to the renewed flourishing of agriculture in the Land of Israel as a portent of impending redemption.

58. Ezek. 36:8–11. This is the prooftext cited in Sanhedrin 98a (see note 57 above).

אבל במידת התמלאות הסאה של גערת ד' ותוכחתו, שהיא מירקה לא רק את היחידים – שהם שבו ברובם בימי הגלות הראשונים – כי אם את רוח האומה בכללה, ותרומם אתו יחד את רוח הארץ אשר נשפל בימי הרעה, במידה זו החלו דרכי ציון האבלות לבקש את תפקידן. העם אשר נעזב מהן החל לחשוב על דבר חפץ שובו אל עריו ואל ארצו, למצוא שמה חיים שלמים, חיים הממלאים את כל הפגום מצד החומר והרוח גם יחד. רק זה מקרוב החל הרוח לפעם, במסתרים בא, עוד סתר פנים לו, מיודעיו הרבים לא יוכלו להכירו ויודעיו לא חזו ימיו. אף אם נראה מראשית צמיחתו בחזון לב לקדושי רוח, ראוהו ולא הכירוהו בעוזו וממשותו, עד אשר במסיבות התהפך והנהו הולך ונגלה. השדרות הקרובות יותר לחפצים חומריים הנן ראשונות להכיר את פעמיו. תכונתו, המלאה עניין לחפצים חומריים, חפץ הארץ, העבודה, הסדר והמשטר החברתי, לא זרה היא לרוחם כמו לרוח בני עלייה המיוחדים של עם ממושך וממורט, אשר שכח חיים ונשה טובה.

וכאן אנשי לב נתבעים לבוא לעמוד במערכה, לחזק ידיים רפות, לרומם רוח כל מתייאש ולאמץ כל כושל, לקרוא בקול גדול: "ציון, אל ירפו ידיך!". הנה נשמת אלהים חיים העלומה, אשר ישבה בסתר המדרגה בכל ימי הגלות, הולכת ומתגלה. את הודה ויפעתה הלוא לא תוכל לגלות רק בעמה החי חיים שלמים על אדמתו. כשם שאין השכינה שורה באיש יחידי אלא על גיבור ועשיר ובעל קומה, אלא שכל זה לא יסכון מאומה בלתי המעלות הרוחניות של חכמה וענווה, כך אין השכינה הכללית שורה אלא בעם מלא גבורה, עושר וקוממיות, אלא שכל אלה ימצאו את ערכם רק בהיעשותם בסיסים להאור הרוחני האלהי, הממולא אור ד' וענוות צדק.

בנפש נדהמה ובברכיים כושלות מעוצר רעה ויגון, של עקת אויב ושפלות נדודים, באפס תקווה וניחומים באדמת נכר, באו אל הארץ פזורי גולה, שרידים יחידים. עיניהם הטרוטות, מרוב אפלה של גולה אחר גולה, לא תוכלנה עוד

corruptions would have been likely to return and reawaken. So their spiritual vision was blocked, and most people forgot about the land, and the scattered individuals who were concerned with it related to it as a spiritual ideal rather than as a physical reality.

But with the fulfillment of the whole measure of God's rebuke (which refines not just individuals, who began to return from the early days of the exile, but also the spirit of the nation as a whole, which lifts up with it the degraded spirit of the land), the mourning for Zion began to seek outlets in action. The people that felt itself abandoned by Zion began to conceive the desire to return to its city and its land, to find there a life that would be more whole, in which the spiritual and physical could be healed simultaneously. Then the spirit began secretly to beat again, imperceptibly to most people – "Even those close to Him cannot foresee His actions."[59] Even if this initial growth was apparent to those with seeing hearts and holy souls, they saw yet did not recognize its strength and substance, until they turned around and there it was – revealing itself. Those tendrils of new life that were closest to material urges were the first to show perceptible traces. The desire for land, for physical work, for social organization were not strange to the most exalted spirits of this long-suffering people that had generally forgotten the ways of physical existence and that was indebted for its material support to others.

Now we need dauntless people to step forward. They must strengthen the weak of spirit, raise up the despairing, support the falling, and declare loudly, "Zion: do not give up!" The spirit of the living, hidden God, concealed throughout the exile is being revealed. It can fully appear only in a people living a holistic life on its own land. Just as with individuals, the divine presence rests only on one who is strong, self-sufficient, and dignified, as well as possessing spiritual qualities of wisdom and humility, so, too, the divine presence rests only on the people collectively when they are strong, materially self-sufficient, and upright (these qualities, however, find their true value when they serve as a basis for the flourishing of a godly spirit, filled with the light of righteous humility).

59. Job 24:1.

לסבול את כל תוקף האור הגדול הזורע בארץ. הקומה עוד לא נזדקפה, הרוח עוד לא נתעודד, הנשמה האלהית עוד לא נגלתה בתעופת עווה. אבל קווים בודדים של אורה פזורים בכל עברים, הקץ המגולה הולך וקרב, וכל אשר רוח ד׳ מפעמו יחוש להיות מהבונים הראשונים הבונים את בניין האומה בארץ חמדת עולמים!

כמו שצעירה היא קוממות עמנו על אדמת הקודש, כמו שדל וקטן הוא בניננו לעומת תקוותנו הגדולה, שהיא נאדרת בימין ה׳ רוממה "לנטוע שמים וליסוד ארץ ולאמר לציון עמי אתה", כן דק וחלוש הוא הרוח המורגש בקרבנו מרוממותה של ארץ חמדה. והדר כבוד אל המתגלה בקדושת היובל והשמיטה על אדמת הקודש, הנותן עוז ותעצומות לעם, רק מרחוק עוד ייראה לנו. אמנם מחיות הן את רוחנו המצוות התלויות בארץ כמה שעולה בידינו לקיים מהן גם כעת, אם כי עדיין אין לנו שום דבר בשלמותו. אבל הגיעה השעה לתחיית התורה המכוונת לעומת תחיית הארץ: תלמודן של המצוות התלויות בארץ החל להיות הולך ונחשב, לכל עם ד׳ המפנה פניו אל ארצו ברוח ד׳ אשר עליו – לחובה קדושה יתר על החובה הכללית המקפת את כל התורה כולה, וביותר החלה חובתו להיגלות על יושבי אדמת הקודש.

תלמוד מביא לידי מעשה, שינון ההלכות בבירור והרחבה, עשות ספרים והרבות מחקר בהן, מביאים את ההכרה והאהבה אל המצוות התלויות בארץ, אשר נשכחו שנות מאות רבות מכללות האומה, ואור ד׳, שבכל אות ואות ובכל פרט ופרט מפרטיה של תורה, מופיע ומעורר את חשק שמירתן בכל פרטיהן, והכרת צדקן וכבודן הולכת ומתרבה לפי הגדלת תורתן והאדרתה.

---

60. Isa. 56:12.

61. Kiddushin 40b. "Learning is greater [than action] because learning leads to action." This is R. Akiva's opinion, cited in the talmudic debate about whether study is greater than deeds. Among the proofs for its statement that learning leads to action, the

Dumbfounded of spirit, knees quaking from the oppression of enemies and humiliating wanderings, devoid of hope or consolation in the lands of strangers, scattered exiles started to arrive in the land. Bleary-eyed from all the darkness of exile after exile, it was hard for them to absorb the great light that they found sown in the land. Their stature is still not upright and their spirits not yet revived, and the spirit of God is not yet revealed in full force. But scattered shafts of spiritual life suggest that the revealed end is coming closer. All in whom the divine spirit resonates feel themselves to be among the pioneering builders who are constructing the nation's home in its beloved, eternal land.

The reestablishment of the people in its holy land is still young, and what has been built until now is minuscule compared to the grandeur of our hope, which is mantled in godly power – "I, who planted the skies and made firm the earth, have said to Zion, you are My people!"[60] So, too, the spiritual revival within us that is starting to raise up our precious country is small and weak. The glory that will appear when shemitta and *yovel* are observed on the holy land still seem far away. Nonetheless, our spirits are lifted by what we *can* fulfill of the mitzvot that are connected to the land, even though what we have is still only partial. Now is the time to revive those aspects of the Torah that speak precisely to the revival of the land: learning about the special mitzvot of the land is becoming more and more significant for all those of God's people who are focusing on what is happening in the land to which God's spirit has returned – where a special holiness must be reflected and revealed by those who are living here, above and beyond the demands that the rest of the Torah makes on us wherever we are.

"Learning leads to action."[61] Studying the halakhot to gain clarity and breadth of understanding, writing books, and expanding research all increase awareness and love of the mitzvot connected to the land, which were forgotten by most of the people for many centuries. The divine

---

Talmud observes that the giving of the Torah preceded the first shemitta by sixty-one years. Through citing this source, Rav Kook expresses the hope that the study of shemitta will lead to its fuller observance, together with an awareness that this might take some time.

והנה עתה הגיעה שנת השמיטה לפי מניין השנים המוחזק אתנו. מרוב דלות מצב יישובנו בארץ הכרח אמנם להסתפק על פי רוב בהוראת שעה, כאשר הוסכם מאז על פי גדולי הדור, אשר נכנסו לתוך עומק מצב היישוב החדש בארצנו הקדושה, ובהרגשה נאמנה חדרו אל ערכו בעתיד, בחושם שלא לבוז ליום קטנות ולדעת כי מאת ד׳ היתה זאת, לתת ניר לעמו על אדמת קדשו להיות לפתח תקווה וצמיחת קרן ישועה, שגדולה היא חובתנו ליישר את מסילתה, לבלי תפגע מכשולים מצד המצוות התלויות בארץ ככל האפשרי. ואין הקב״ה בא בטרוניא עם בריותיו, וכל הנאמר להקל במקום מצווה דרבים ובמקום הפסד מרובה ושעת הדחק - כל אלה חוברו יחד בשאלה זו במידה מרובה כל כך, עד שאין לה דוגמה בכל השאלות אשר נתעוררו בישראל בחקר דין ומשפט, בכל משך הגלות הארוכה. אבל למרות הפקעת המצווה אשר בהוראת שעה זו ישנם כמה גופי הלכות, הנדרשים לשמור ולעשות בפועל. גם נמצאים יראי ד׳ החרדים אל דברו מאוד, אשר מפני קדושת חיבת המצוות התלויות בארץ ומצוות השביעית, שעיני כל ישראל נשואות לקיומה בארץ חמדה, אינם חסים על הפסד וטורח והם נכונים לקיימה בכל כוח - כדין וכמשפט. ברוכים יהיו לד׳ ולעמו.

ולבד זה, התלמוד בעצמו יביא לידי מעשה, שינון ההלכות יחקוק בלבבות את חיובם בלב ומשמיטה לשמיטה יתוספו רבים, אשר בעוז ד׳ בלבבם ירחיבו את גבול המצווה בכל הרחבתה ופרטיה, ובשמחת ישראל בעושיו בהר הקודש העוז והתעצומות אשר לעם ד׳ בעתיד יוסיפו את היכולת לקיומה הגמור והמשוכלל.

62. Rav Kook refers here to the *heter mekhira* device of selling the land for the duration of the shemitta. See the introduction to this volume for background.

63. Hos. 2:17. Rav Kook quotes from the passage that likens Israel's turn to idolatry to a woman's adultery, which he has previously cited in his introduction. This verse describes the lovers' reconciliation. In Hebrew, the phrase is *petaḥ tikva,* which was the name given to one of the first modern agricultural settlements in Israel (founded in 1878) for similar reasons.

light that suffuses every letter of every detail of the Torah awakens in us a desire to carefully observe these commandments in their entirety. Consciousness of their justice and importance will grow as the study of the Torah concerning them becomes greater and more magnificent.

Now the shemitta year has arrived (according to the reckoning that we have). Owing to the poor situation of our settlements in the land, we will have to make do with the temporary expedient that was endorsed some time ago by the greatest authorities of the generation, who understood deeply the situation of the new settlement in our holy land.[62] They had a penetrating sense of what it could become in the future and knew not to belittle its smallness because they understood that plowing these first furrows on our land could be a "gateway of hope"[63] for our people and portend the growth of a salvation that "came from the Lord."[64] They realized their historical obligation to smooth the path of the new settlements and, as much as possible, not to let the mitzvot that are connected to the land be obstacles. God does not make tyrannical and unreasonable demands of His creatures. The circumstances that allow us to be lenient regarding mitzvot pertaining to the whole community when there is the likelihood of significant financial loss, or in a temporary situation of acute need, are all compounded in this case to an extent unparalleled in the annals of legal questions that have arisen throughout our lengthy exile. Despite the suspension of the mitzva (of shemitta) that is entailed by this temporary edict, there are still some halakhot pertaining to shemitta that we are required to observe. And those who are especially God-fearing, whose holy love of the mitzvot connected to the land that we have long yearned to observe is so great, are not deterred by the trouble and loss they may incur through fully observing shemitta as it should be – and they shall be blessed!

In addition, learning itself leads to action. Studying the halakhot will engrave them on our hearts. From one shemitta year to the next, more and more people will be caught up with enthusiasm. With godly

64. Ps. 118:23.

65. Jerusalem. See, e.g., Isa. 56:7.

מרוח ד׳ החופף על עמו וארצו תחל קדושת השמיטה ותפארת זיו כבודה להתפשט על כל רוח ונפש, לכל עם ד׳ ובייחוד ליושבים בצל קודש של ארץ חמדה, בנעימת ידידות עוז אהבתה. ורוח קדושת היובל המסתתר יופיע מאוצר קדשו על קדושת השמיטה, לעורר קרן ישועה וקול שופר לשגב ישע, לעורר ישנים ולעודד גאולים.

לזאת מצאתי לי לחובה להוציא את החוברת הזאת, אשר סידרתיה להלכות שביעית בע״ה.

אקווה לשמו יתברך כי יגדיל תורה ויאדיר ויזכה אותי ואת כל למודי ד׳, וביותר את אחיי אשר אקרא להם נועם אלו תלמידי חכמים שבארץ ישראל, להרחיב דברים על המצוות התלויות בארץ בכלל ועל מצוות שביעית בפרט. ויחד עם העסק בהלכות המעשיות יתכונן הלב בטוב טעם ודעת להשכיל בנועם ד׳ באור דעת אלהים, ברוח מלא עצה וגבורה, והחונן לאדם דעת הנותן אור חכמה על אדמת קדשו, אשר זיכנו להסתופף בחבל נחלתו, ימלאנו רוח דעה ויחזקנו בשכל טוב, ויצילנו מכל שגיאה, למען עמו ונחלתו. ומהרה ייאמנו דבריו לנביאו:

> ולקחתי אתכם מן הגוים וקבצתי אתכם מכל הארצות, והבאתי אתכם אל אדמתכם, וזרקתי עליכם מים טהורים וטהרתם מכל טומאותיכם, ומכל גלוליכם אטהר אתכם. ונתתי לכם לב חדש ורוח חדשה אתן בקרבכם, והסירתי את לב האבן מבשרכם ונתתי לכם לב בשר. ואת רוחי אתן בקרבכם, ועשיתי את אשר בחקי תלכו ומשפטי תשמרו ועשיתם, וישבתם בארץ אשר נתתי לאבותיכם, והייתם לי לעם ואנכי אהיה לכם לאלהים. והושעתי אתכם מכל טומאותיכם, וקראתי אל הדגן והרביתי אותו ולא אתן עליכם רעב. והרביתי את פרי העץ ותנובת השדה, למען אשר לא תקחו עוד חרפת רעב בגוים (יחזקאל ל״ו, כ״ד-ל׳).

66. Ezek. 36:24–30.

boldness in their hearts, they will broaden the fulfillment of the mitzva in all its details. The fierce joy that will be generated by Israel observing the shemitta on the holy mountain[65] will lead, in the future, to its complete and all-encompassing fulfillment.

The holiness of shemitta will emanate from the spirit of God that hovers over His people and land and spread to all life – to all God's people and especially to those who live in the holy shelter of this precious land, in the sweet companionship of its loving refuge. The spirit of the Jubilee, which lies latent, will appear from within the storehouse of holiness that is in the shemitta, and the sound of the shofar will herald salvation, rousing the sleepy and encouraging the recently redeemed.

That is why I felt obliged to write this book laying out the halakhot of shemitta, with God's help.

I hope to God that through it, the Torah will be made great and glorious; that I and all those who yearn to learn of God's ways, especially my brothers, whom I call upon in pleasantness, the great Torah scholars of the Land of Israel, will merit to expand our teaching about the mitzvot that concern the land, and especially shemitta. And alongside our involvement in the practical halakhot, may our hearts be strengthened with wisdom and discernment to know, with a spirit that is filled with counsel and strength, the light of divine knowledge that is being granted to our holy land, which we have been fortunate to inherit; and may this spirit of this knowledge fill and strengthen us with sound understanding and save us from errors for the sake of His people and inheritance. May God's word to the prophets be soon fulfilled:

> I will take you from among the nations and gather you from all countries, and I will bring you back to your land. I will sprinkle clean water upon you and you shall be clean: I will cleanse you from all your uncleanness and all your fetishes. And I will give you a new heart and put a new spirit into you: I will remove the heart of stone from your body and give you a heart of flesh; and I will put My spirit into you. Thus I will cause you to follow My laws and faithfully to observe My rules. Then you shall dwell in the land that I gave to your fathers, and you shall be My people and I will be your God. And when I have delivered you from all

כה אמר ד׳ אלהים: ביום טהרי אתכם מכל עונותיכם והושבתי את הערים ונבנו החרבות, והארץ הנשמה תעבד, תחת אשר היתה שממה לעיני כל עובר. ואמרו: הארץ הלזו הנשמה היתה כגן עדן, והערים החרבות והנשמות והנהרסות בצורות ישבו, וידעו הגוים אשר ישארו סביבותיכם, כי אני ד׳ בניתי הנהרסות, נטעתי הנשמה, אני ד׳ דברתי ועשיתי (שם, ל״ג-ל״ו).

(עיה״ק יפו ת״ו, התר״ע)

your uncleanness, I will summon the grain and make it abundant, and I will not bring famine upon you. I will make the fruit of your trees and the crops of your fields abundant, so that you shall never again be humiliated before the nations because of the famine.[66]

Thus said the Lord, God: when I have cleansed you of all your iniquities, I will people your settlements, and the ruined places shall be rebuilt; and the desolate land, after lying waste in the sight of every passerby, shall again be tilled. And men shall say, "That land, once desolate, has now become like the garden of Eden; and the cities, once ruined, desolate, and ravaged, are now populated and fortified." And the nations that are left around you shall know that I the Lord have rebuilt the ravaged places and replanted the desolate land. I the Lord have spoken and will act.[67]

The Holy City of Jaffa, may it be built and established, 1909

67. Ezek. 36:33–36.

שבת הארץ / הלכות

מאת הרב ר' אברהם יצחק הכהן קוק זצ"ל

Selected Halakhot from *Shabbat HaAretz*

Rabbi Abraham Isaac Kook

Introductory Note

The selections from the halakhic sections of *Shabbat HaAretz* have been made to illustrate the principal elements of Rav Kook's case for the *heter mekhira* leniency that were surveyed in the introductory essay. As selections, they are necessarily a partial sample of the work, and do not represent the entirety of his complex argument. The first resort for resolving obscurities should be the original, whole text.

Though best known today as a philosopher and mystic, Rav Kook was also one of the leading *poskim*, halakhic decisors, of his day. These excerpts convey some of his remarkable erudition, creativity, and boldness as a halakhic thinker. An account of his encompassing approach to halakhic decision-making is beyond the scope of this book.[1]

1. Important contributions to understanding Rav Kook's approach to halakha include: Arye Edrei, "From Orthodoxy to Religious Zionism: Rabbi Kook and the Sabbatical Year Polemic," trans. Shmuel Peerless, http://www2.tau.ac.il/InternetFiles/news/UserFiles//Shemitta.pdf (2008); Michael Z. Nahorai, "Halakhah, Metahalakhah and the Redemption of Israel; Reflections on the Rabbinic Rulings of Rav Kook," in *Rabbi Abraham Isaac Kook and Jewish Spirituality*, ed. Lawrence J. Kaplan and David Shatz (New York: New York University Press, 1995); Avinoam Rosenak, *The Prophetic Halakhah: Rabbi A. I. H. Kook's Philosophy of Halakhah* (Hebrew) (Jerusalem: Magnes Press, 2005); and Neriya Gutel, *Innovation in Tradition: The Halakhic-Philosophical Teachings of Rabbi Kook* (Hebrew) (Jerusalem: Magnes Press, 2005).

וזאת למודעי

כל הדברים, אשר הרציתי ב״מבוא״ להמליץ על אחינו יושבי אדמת קדשנו ת״ו הסומכים על ההיתר הנהוג משמיטות שעברו, על פי הוראת חכמים שמצאו את הדבר נכון להורות בו הלכה למעשה להוראת שעה, לא באו כי אם להודיע שלא להשוות את העובדים הללו – העושים את מעשיהם על פי הוראה מסודרת – לעוברי חוק תוה״ק חלילה. וכן למען חזק את רבים מאחינו פזורי הגולה, הכמהים לבוא ולהיאחז בארץ חמדה אם רק יראה להם דרך איך להתפרנס מעמל כפיהם, ופוחדים הם מפני הפסק העבודה בשביעית בזמן הזה, אשר ברכת ד׳ עודנה חבויה עד בוא עת היגלותה ב״ב, ובייחוד אותם החפצים להשקיע סכומי כסף גדולים לכונן פרדסים, כרמים, שדי תבואה, גני חמד, שהם דואגים מאוד מפני שביתת המסחר והפסק חיבורו בשביעית, שעל ידי זה לא יוכל להתכונן במידה הגונה גם בכל ימות השנים כולם. מתוך כך אלה ואלה מושכים את ידיהם מארץ הקודש ומשקעים עצמם בארץ העמים, וקדושת חמדת ישיבת ארץ הקודש ובניינה נעזבת מהם. לפיכך מצאתי לנפשי חובה, לבאר את תוכן ההיתר הנהוג על פי ההפקעה בעת ההכרח, למען דעת, שאם יידרש הכרח ישיבת ארץ הקודש להתנהג בו, הרי הדבר ערוך ונכון על פי יסודות נאמנים, וחלילה לעזוב משום זה את חמדת ארץ צבי, ומעלות בקודש העליונות...

2. This refers to the leniency of selling the land to non-Jews for the duration of the sabbatical year, justification of which is the subject of this text. This leniency was invoked as a one-off expedient to permit struggling Jewish farmers to continue working during the sabbatical years of 1888–9, 1895–6 and 1902–3. However, it became increasingly controversial and was attacked as a legal fiction. In this work Rav Kook endeavors to place the leniency on firm foundations.

NOTICE OF INTENT

All the matters that I set out in this "Introduction" to recommend concerning our brothers dwelling in our Holy Land, may it be built and established, who rely upon the leniency [*heter*] that has been practiced in recent sabbatical years [*shemittot*; sing. *shemitta*],[2] according to the teaching of scholars who saw fit to teach it as a practical rule and temporary ruling [*lehorot bo halakha lemaaseh lehoraat shaa*], are intended to show that there is no comparison whatsoever between these workers – who act according to an established ruling – and those who simply break the statute [*ḥok*] of our Holy Torah, God forbid. They are also meant to strengthen our brethren who are scattered in the Diaspora and yearn to come and to take their place in this precious land if they could only see a way to make a living here by the labor of their hands.[3] They are afraid of the interruption to their work in the sabbatical year when God's full blessing remains concealed until the time of our redemption, may it come speedily in our days. In particular, there are those who wish to invest large sums to establish orchards, vineyards, fields, and gardens, but are very concerned that the cessation of trade during the sabbatical year could impede their ability to plan properly for the other years. Therefore, both groups are withdrawing their efforts from the Holy Land and investing in foreign countries; the holy delight to settle the Holy Land and develop it has left them. So I felt obliged to clarify the nature of the leniency that people customarily follow that works by temporarily suspending [*hafkaa*] [the ownership and thus the holiness of the land] when necessary. One may thus know that if the necessity of settling the Holy Land requires him to avail himself of this leniency, it is sound and grounded on reliable foundations. God forbid that anyone should for this reason abandon our beautiful country, with its extraordinary level of holiness....

3. This text was written on the eve of the 1909–10 sabbatical year, in the midst of the Second Aliyah wave of Jewish immigration to Ottoman-ruled Palestine, which began in 1904 and ended with the outbreak of World War I in 1914.

אבל חלילה וחלילה לדון מזה איזו התרשלות מקיום המצווה הקדושה והחביבה הזאת, לכל אשר נתן ד׳ רוח טהרה בלבבו ודי אומץ וביטחון בנפשו לעשות ולקיים את כל פרשת דבר השמיטה, כהלכתה וכמאמרה. ברוך יהיה לד׳ שוכן ציון, החפץ בארץ חמדה ובקדושת מצוותיה התלויות בה, אשר בהם אוצר חביון גנוז ושורש גאולת עולמים לגוי קדוש על אדמת הקודש.

וכגון דא ודאי אין צריך למודעי, שלא יימצא שום יחיד או מוסד, שישתמש בדברינו, לכוף חס ושלום, לעבוד בשביעית, אפילו על פי סדרי ההיתר בדרך ההפקעה, את אלה אנשי לב אשר רוח אהבת ד׳ וחמדת מצוותיו נוססה בהם, והם רוצים בכל לבם לשמור ולקיים את מצוות השמיטה כמאמרה בלא שום דרכי הקולות שנאמרו מפני דוחק השעה. ובוודאי ידעו גם אלה אשר תעלה בידם שמירת המצווה במילואה לדון לכף זכות בכל רגשי כבוד ואהבת ישראל, את כל אלה שמצבם בפרט או מצב היישוב בכלל מכריח אותם להתנהג על פי סדרי ההיתר וההפקעה, "ואיש את רעת רעהו אל תחשבו בלבבכם... והאמת והשלום אהבו".

But conversely, God forbid that one should infer from my words any [license for] negligence in fulfilling this holy, beloved commandment by one to whom God grants sufficient purity of heart and courage of spirit and faith to do and to fulfill the whole of the sabbatical year according to its rules and as it was spoken [*kehilkhata ukhemaamara*]. He will be blessed by the Lord who dwells in Zion, who loves His precious land and the holiness of the commandments that depend upon it, a land in which reside latent, hidden treasures and the root of eternal redemption for a holy nation on the Holy Land.

It goes without saying that no individual or institution should use our words to compel anyone to work during the sabbatical year, even within the provisions of this leniency. [No one should force] those with willing hearts in whom the spirit of the love of God and desire for the commandments flutters, who sincerely wish to observe and to fulfill the sabbatical year as it was spoken without any of the leniencies that were propounded because of temporary exigencies. Know also that, of course, all those who succeed in observing the commandment fully should judge favorably and with feelings of complete respect and love for Israel those whose individual situation or the collective situation of the settlement [in the Land of Israel] compels them to act according to the leniency of temporary suspension: "And do not contrive evil against one another...but you must love honesty and integrity."[4]

4. Zech. 8:17, 19.

מבוא

[א]
משמעות סוגיית הגמרא, שהלכה פסוקה כרבי ששביעית בזמן הזה דרבנן

פשטם של דברי הסוגיא דמועד קטן (ב׳ ע״ב) מורה, שעל דברי רבי, שאומר: ״בשתי שמיטות הכתוב מדבר, אחת שמיטת קרקע ואחת שמיטת כספים – בזמן שאתה משמט קרקע אתה משמט כספים ובזמן שאי אתה משמט קרקע אי אתה משמט בספים״ – אין על זה שום מחלוקת, שכוונתו במה שאמר ״אין אתה משמט כספים״ היינו שאין נוהג אז דין שמיטה, שבה יש השמטת כספים, שזהו מבדיל את השמיטה מן היובל מה שביובל אין השמטת כספים נוהגת, והשביעית משמטת כספים...

על כל פנים זהו פשוט, לכאורה, שכוונת הברייתא דרבי – ״בזמן שאי אתה משמט קרקע אי אתה משמט כספים״ – שבכלל שביעית אין נוהגת אז מן התורה, לא שמיטת כספים שהיא מיוחדת ומבוארת ביחוד בשביעית, ולא לכל דיני שמיטת קרקע ועבודותיה. וזה אין לומר, שכוונת הברייתא היא רק להוציא שמיטת כספים ממש, שאינה נוהגת מן התורה אלא בזמן שהיובל נוהג, אבל בכל דיני שביעית בעבודת הארץ נוהג האיסור גם בזמן הזה לדעת רבי, שהרי

---

5. R. Yehuda the Prince, a leading second-century sage in the Land of Israel to whom tradition attributes the compilation of the Mishna.
6. See Lev. 25.
7. See Deut. 15:1–10.
8. Rebbe infers from Deut. 15:2 that the two major areas of the sabbatical year, the sabbatical for agriculture and for debt relief are interdependent in their application. See Rashi ad loc., s.v. *bizman*.
9. The Jubilee year, which was marked by a return of land holding to the original owners, occurred at the end of seven cycles of sabbatical years. See Lev. 25.

Preface

1. The meaning of the passage in the Talmud, that the rule is decided like Rebbe that the sabbatical year at this time is of rabbinic authority

The plain meaning of the passage in Moed Katan (2b) teaches that there is no dispute regarding the following statement of Rebbe:[5] "Scripture speaks of two kinds of release [*shemitta*]: release of land[6] and release of loans.[7] In a period when land is released [*meshamet karka*], so too loans are released [*meshamet kesafim*]. In a period when land is not released, neither are loans released."[8] [Rebbe's] intention in saying "neither are loans released" is that [all] the laws of the sabbatical year, which include the remission of loans, are now not in effect. This is a distinction between the sabbatical year and the Jubilee, in that remission of loans applies to the sabbatical year, but not to the Jubilee....[9]

In any case, it is obvious that the intention of Rebbe's *baraita*,[10] "in a period when land is not released, neither are loans released," is that the sabbatical year as a whole was not then applicable according to the Torah,[11] neither for the remission of loans, which is specifically explained to be unique to the sabbatical year, nor for all the laws [*dinei*] of releasing the land and agricultural work [which apply also to the Jubilee year]. This is not to say that the *baraita* means to exclude specifically the remission of loans – that according to Rebbe, [the remission of loans]

10. A *baraita* is a rabbinic statement that is contemporaneous with the Mishna but not included in it.

11. The distinction between laws that have the force of a direct Torah obligation (*de'oraita*) and those that have the lesser force of an obligation based on the authority

על קושיית הגמרא שם במועד קטן: "אלא שביעית בין למאן דאמר משום חורש בין למאן דאמר משום זורע – חרישה וזריעה בשביעית מי שרי" – מתרץ על זה אביי בפשיטות: בשביעית בזמן הזה ורבי היא וכו'. ואין לומר, שזוהי רק דעת אביי לבדו, אבל רבא חולק על זה בפשט דברי רבי, דאם כן למה מתרץ רבא שם את המשנה במועד קטן אליבא דרבנן דווקא? הלוא היה לו לומר שאפילו רבי לא סבירא ליה שבזמן הזה דרבנן רק שמיטת כספים ולא איסור עבודת הארץ... אלא ודאי פשוט הוא, שאליבא דרבי בין אביי בין רבא כולי עלמא מודים ששביעית בזמן הזה לכל פרטיה היא דרבנן, בין בשמיטת כספים בין באיסור עבודת קרקע, מפני שדעת רבי היא ששמיטה ויובל תלויים הם זה בזה מן התורה.

ולפי מה דקיימא לן כסוגיא דגיטין (ל"ו) דתקנתא דהלל בפרוזבול, שהיא הלכה פסוקה ולכולי עלמא אתיא היא אליבא דרבי... על כל פנים הלוא לכולי עלמא הלכה פסוקה כרבי. שכן מורה באמת הרצאת לשון הסוגיא... וכן נראה מתוך התכת הלשון, שגם רבא מסכים לדינא דשביעית בזמן הזה דרבנן – מתוך שהוא מתרץ את הקושיא הנופלת על דעה זו.

---

of the rabbis (*derabanan*) is a critical one in Jewish law in general and in this text of Rav Kook's in particular. It is crucial to his purpose to show that shemitta in post-exilic times is merely of rabbinical authority, as a basis for his lenient rulings.

12 The Mishna (Moed Katan 2a) stated conditions under which one may water an irrigated field during the intermediate days of a festival (Ḥol HaMoed) or during shemitta. The Talmud then asked how it is possible that watering a field can be permitted in the shemitta year, because sowing and plowing (which make watering necessary) are both forbidden in the sabbatical. Abaye answered that the Mishna refers to the contemporary reality in which shemitta is of rabbinic authority, which is the opinion of Rebbe. Consequently the Mishna permits watering where necessary to avoid serious financial loss.

13. The root of Rebbe's opinion that shemitta in his time was only observed on rabbinic authority lay in his understanding of the interdependence of the sabbatical and Jubilee cycles. The Jubilee was no longer practiced since a significant minority of Jews no longer lived in Israel (based on Lev. 25:10) Consequently, Rebbe inferred that shemitta, which was inherently connected to the Jubilee, no longer had the force of a Torah commandment in his time, but was only practiced based on rabbinic authority. (See Arakhin 32b.)

14. The *prozbul* was an enactment of the first-century rabbi Hillel the Elder that circumvented the biblical requirement (see Deut. 15:2) to remit loans in the sabbatical year. The Torah mandates that loans be forgiven at the end of each shemitta year (Deut. 15:2). However, Hillel noted that in his time this law was deterring lenders

is only applicable according to the Torah when the Jubilee is applicable, whereas regarding the sabbatical laws of agricultural work, the prohibition is applicable even now. For in response to the Talmud's question in Moed Katan (2b), "According to both the opinion that [watering seeds on the Intermediate Days of a Festival] is forbidden because of [the prohibition on] plowing and according to the opinion that it is forbidden because of [the prohibition on] sowing, are plowing and sowing in the sabbatical year allowed?"[12] Abaye answers simply, "This speaks of the sabbatical year in our time, and the statement is according to Rebbe...." And one cannot say that this is only the opinion of Abaye, and that Rava argues about the meaning of Rebbe's words. For if this were so, then why does Rava explain the Mishna in Moed Katan, as specifically following the opinion of the rabbis (and not of Rebbe)? Rava should rather have said that even Rebbe only thinks that shemitta in our times is of rabbinic authority with respect to the remission of debts, but not with respect to the prohibition of agricultural work.... So clearly both Abaye and Rava agree that, according to Rebbe, the sabbatical year in our time is, in all its details, of rabbinic authority [*derabanan*]. [This is the case] both concerning remission of loans and the prohibitions on agricultural work, because Rebbe is of the opinion that the Torah stipulates the interdependence of the sabbatical year and the Jubilee.[13]

This can also be seen according to our understanding of the passage in Gittin (36b), that Hillel's enactment of the *prozbul*,[14] which is a decided rule [*halakha pesuka*], and according to everyone it results from Rebbe's opinion [that the sabbatical year in our time is a rabbinic commandment]...it is evident from the flow of the language in the passage that Rava also agrees that the sabbatical year in our times is of rabbinic authority, because he responds to a problem that follows from that premise.

---

from making loans as shemitta approached, to the detriment of the poor and needy who were meant to be helped by the remission of loans! He therefore innovated the *prozbul* device, under which lenders could submit their loan papers to a court, which would collect their debts for them. (The court's authority to do this was grounded in its power to declare property ownerless, according to the principle of *hefker beit din hefker*, in order to advance desirable social and religious goals.)

אם כן, משתי הסוגיות האלו ביחד אנו מוצאים, שהלכה פסוקה היא כרבי, דשביעית בזמן הזה, גם בעבודת הארץ, היא רק מדרבנן.

וכך היא שיטת התוספות שם בסוגיאן דגיטין...

[יא]
יסוד היתר המכירה - אם יש קניין לנכרי להפקיע או לא, מחלוקת הב"י והמבי"ט בדין קדושת שביעית בשל נכרים

יסוד היתר המכירה הוא בעיקרו על פי רוב קמאי ובתראי, דסבירא להו ששביעית בזמן הזה דרבנן, שזהו יסוד דברי רש"י (סנהדרין כ"ו א', ד"ה אגיסטון), שבקרקע של נכרי מותר לחרוש ולעשות כל עבודה, וכך היא דעת הר"ח בפירושו שם, כמבואר למעיין בדבריו כמו שביארתי מזה בקונטרס אחרון, וכן דעת בעלי התוספות והערוך והפוסקים הסוברים שהיא בזמן הזה מדרבנן. שהרי פשוט הוא בסוגיא דגמרא (גיטין מ"ז א'), דהא דאמר רבה שאין קניין לנכרי בארץ ישראל להפקיע מידי מעשר הוא דווקא במידי דאורייתא, אבל במידי דרבנן אמרינן יש קניין לנכרי להפקיע...

---

15. Gittin 36a, s.v. *Mi Ikah*. *Tosafot* is the name collectively applied to a group of talmudic commentators active principally in France and Germany between the twelfth and fourteenth centuries. Their commentary appears on the page of the standard, Vilna printed edition of the Talmud, opposite Rashi's commentary.
16. *Beit Yosef* refers to Rabbi Yosef Karo (1488–1575), author of the authoritative halakhic code, the *Shulḥan Arukh*. (*Beit Yosef* was the title of his earlier halakhic work.)
17. Mabit is an acronym for Rabbi Moshe di Trani (1505–85), a prominent halakhic authority who, like Rabbi Karo, lived in Safed. The dispute between the two over

We find, therefore, from both of these talmudic passages that the rule is decided according to Rebbe: The sabbatical year [including the remission of loans], as well as agricultural work, in our times, is only of rabbinic authority.

This also is the opinion of *Tosafot.*...[15]

11. The foundation for the leniency to sell the land: whether the acquisition of a non-Jew suspends [the obligation of the sabbatical year] or not; the dispute between *Beit Yosef*[16] and Mabit[17] over the holiness of the sabbatical year [of land in Israel that is owned] by non-Jews [*nokhrim*]

The foundation for the leniency of selling [the land] is fundamentally, according to most of the earlier and later authorities, that the sabbatical year in our time is of rabbinic authority. This is the basis for Rashi's[18] statement (Sanhedrin 26a, s.v. *agiston*) that [a Jew] may plow and do all sorts of agricultural work [during the sabbatical year] on the land of a non-Jew. This is also the opinion of Rabbenu Ḥananel[19] in his commentary (ad loc.) as will be clear to those who study his words as I have explained them [...]; it is also the opinion of Tosafot and *Arukh*,[20] and those decisors who believe that the sabbatical year in our times is of rabbinic authority. For this is clear in the discussion in Gittin (47a): Rabba's statement that the acquisition by a non-Jew of land in Israel does not exempt [*lehafkiyaa*] that land from [the obligation of] tithes is specifically about a biblical [commandment]. Concerning a rabbinic [commandment], however, the acquisition of land by a non-Jew does exempt the land [from that commandment]....

---

whether or not purchase of land in Israel by a non-Jew suspends the holiness of the land and the consequent obligation to observe the laws of shemitta, was of foundational importance for determining the viability of the *heter mekhira*.

18. Abbreviation of Rabbi Shlomo Yitzhaki (1040–1105), the preeminent medieval talmudic commentator.
19. Hananel Ben Hushiel, 990–1053, a prominent North African talmudic commentator.
20. A talmudic dictionary, compiled by Nathan ben Yehiel (1035–1106).

מכל מקום בקדושה זו של שביעית יש קניין לנכרי להפקיע כיוון שקדושה זו היא מדרבנן.

והנה יסוד שיטת הב"י, שפירות של נכרים אין בהם משום קדושת שביעית, הוא משום שסובר שדעת הרמב"ם היא, דהא דאמרינן אין קניין לנכרי בארץ ישראל אינו אלא שאם ישראל חזר וקנה ממנו, אז אינו נחשב ככיבוש יחיד, ואין דינה כסוריא אלא כגוף עיקר ארץ ישראל. אבל כל זמן שהיא ביד הנכרי הרי היא מופקעת מקדושתה; ומטי לה מדברי הרמב"ם (ה' תרומות פ"ד). אמנם מדיוק לשון הרמב"ם (ה' שמיטה פ"ד הכ"ט): "נכרי שקנה קרקע בארץ ישראל וזרעה בשביעית פירותיה מותרין, שלא גזרו על הספיחין אלא מפני עוברי עבירה – והנכרים אינם מצווים על השביעית כדי שנגזור עליהם", משמע לו מזה להכסף משנה, שעיקר הטעם הוא מפני שזורעה הגוי בקרקע שלו והווי תרתי למעליותא: הקרקע היא של נכרי והמלאכה נעשתה על ידי נכרי, ומשמע הא אם היתה הזריעה על ידי ישראל, אף על פי שהקרקע היא של נכרי, הפירות אסורין. ולכאורה קשה כיוון שסובר, שכל זמן שהקרקע היא ביד הנכרי היא מופקעת מקדושתה, אם כן הרי היא לגבי חובת המצוות כחוץ לארץ, ולמה לא תהיה העבודה מותרת לישראל – וכמו שבאמת כך היא שיטתם של רש"י, הר"ח, הערוך, תוספות לחד שינויא, בעלי התוספות והלכות ארץ ישראל – ולמה דייק הרמב"ם דווקא כשזורעה הגוי והלוא גם כשזורעה ישראל היה הדין נותן להתיר הפירות? לפיכך נראה לומר, דסבר הרמב"ם שחכמים אסרו לחזק ידי

21. I.e., *Beit Yosef* understands Maimonides' statement "there is no acquisition of land by a non-Jew in Israel" to mean merely that the non-Jew's purchase does not derogate from the full "Land of Israel" status of the land after a Jew repurchases it.

22. *Kesef Mishneh* is a commentary on Maimonides' *Mishneh Torah* authored by Rabbi Yosef Karo, who also wrote the *Beit Yosef* and the *Shulḥan Arukh*.

23. Rav Kook infers that since the *Kesef Mishneh* notes two distinct halakhic advantages to the situation where the non-Jew is sowing his own land (i.e., the non-Jew owns the land and in addition performs the labor), if only one of these applied (e.g., a Jew had done the work in a non-Jew's field during shemitta), then according to *Kesef Mishneh*, Maimonides would not have permitted the produce.

24. Rav Kook notes a contradiction between the inference regarding Rabbi Karo's view as expressed in his *Kesef Mishneh* explained in footnote 27 below, and Rabbi Karo's view as described here that "so long as the land is in the non-Jew's hands, its holiness

Nevertheless, concerning the holiness of the sabbatical year, holiness by rabbinic authority is suspended when the land is purchased by a non-Jew. . . .

The basis of *Beit Yosef*'s position that the produce of [land owned by] a non-Jew does not possess the sanctity of the sabbatical year lies in his understanding of Maimonides' view. [According to him, Maimonides' view is that] when it is said [in the Talmud], "A non-Jew cannot acquire in the Land of Israel," this only means that if a Jew buys the land back from the non-Jew, this [repurchase] is not considered to be "an act of individual conquest," and it is not [thus] treated like Syria but rather as an integral part of the Land of Israel.[21] But so long as the land is in the non-Jew's hands, its holiness is suspended; *Beit Yosef* infers this from the words of Maimonides in [*Mishneh Torah,*] "Laws of Priestly Gifts," 4 [:15]. However, from a close reading of Maimonides' statement ([*Mishneh Torah,*] "Laws of the Sabbatical Year and Jubilee," 4:29), "If a non-Jew buys land in Israel and sows it in the sabbatical year, the fruits may be eaten, because the decree against eating produce that grows by itself was only made in order [to deter] transgressors, but non-Jews are not commanded to keep the laws of the sabbatical year [at all], so they are not covered by this decree," *Kesef Mishneh*[22] infers from this that the essential reason [that the produce is permitted] is that the non-Jew is sowing in his own field, and that this carries two advantages: first, the land belongs to the non-Jew, and second, the work is done by a non-Jew. This thus implies that if the sowing was done by a Jew, even though the land was owned by a non-Jew, the produce would still be forbidden.[23] This seems problematic since [*Kesef Mishneh*] apparently believes that so long as the land is in the hands of the non-Jew, its holiness is suspended. But if as regards to the obligation of the commandments, it has the same status as land outside Israel, why should work done by a Jew not be permitted?[24] This is in fact the opinion of Rashi, Rabbenu Ḥananel, *Arukh, Tosafot,* and the author of "Laws of the Land of Israel." Why, then, does Maimonides specify a case where the non-Jew sows the

is suspended." *Kesef Mishneh*'s implicit opinion that if a Jew did work in a non-Jew's field in the shemitta the produce is not permitted means that non-Jewish ownership does *not* suspend the holiness of the land.

הגוי יותר מבדברים בעלמא, כדפסק כן הרמב״ם (פ״ח ה״ח) וכמו שכתבנו לעיל, אבל לסייעו בידיים אסור, ונראה שאסרו זה להרחיק את ישראל מעבודת השדה בשביעית, כדי שלא יבוא לעבוד בתוך שדהו, לכן אם היה הישראל בעצמו זורע שדה של גוי בשביעית, כיוון שעבר על דברי חכמים, ראוי לאסור משום קנס. ולפי זה נאמר, שכל פלוגתתם, של הרמב״ם וספר התרומות וסיעתו, היא רק במידי דרבנן, דמן התורה הרי סובר גם הרמב״ם, שכל זמן שהיא ביד גוי היא מופקעת מקדושתה, אלא שגזירת חכמים היא שלא לחזק את ידם במעשה, ולכן אסור לישראל לעבוד בקרקע זו, ולדעת בעלי התוספות אין כאן שום איסור, דמוקי הא דאין עודרין עם הנכרי דווקא למאן דאמר שביעית בזמן הזה דאורייתא ואין קניין לנכרי להפקיע, וסובר שאינו מפקיע אפילו כשהיא תחת ידו, אבל בזמן הזה שיש קניין להפקיע, אין איסור כלל לחזקו ומותר גם לעדור עמו ולעבוד הישראל בעצמו בשדהו של נכרי – ועל כל פנים נראה, שמחלוקת שלהם היא ספיקא במידי דרבנן, דמן התורה גם להרמב״ם אין שום איסור כשיעבוד ישראל בקרקע המופקעת מקדושתה, כל זמן שהיא תחת יד הנכרי.

[יב]
איסור ״לא תחנם״ במכירת קרקע לנכרי

בעניין ״לא תחנם״, שאסור למכור לגוי קרקע בארץ ישראל, יפה העיר חד מבי דינא הרה״ג ר״ז שך נ״י, דיש לומר דבגוי שבלאו הכי יש לו חניה בקרקע אין

25. The question assumes the *Beit Yosef*'s opinion that non-Jewish ownership of the land suspends its holiness and seeks to understand the *Kesef Mishneh*'s apparently contradictory view.

26. Maimonides codifies the gemara from Gittin 62a that limits the Mishna's statement (Gittin 61a) "we may lend support to idolaters who work in the shemitta year" to offering verbal encouragement; actively supporting the idolater's work in the shemitta year is forbidden.

27. Rav Kook resolves the apparent contradiction within Rabbi Karo's view between the *Beit Yosef* and the *Kesef Mishneh* by understanding the latter as forbidding the produce of a Jew's work in a non-Jew's field as a penalty for the Jew's actively supporting the idolater's work; thus understood, *Kesef Mishneh* does not undermine *Beit Yosef*'s view that non-Jewish ownership suspends the holiness of the land.

28. I.e., on the question of whether or not the rabbis penalized produce grown through the labor of Jews on non-Jewish-owned land during shemitta.

land? Surely [on this view] if a Jew did the sowing, the produce would be permitted as well.[25] Apparently, Maimonides thought that the sages prohibited anything more than verbal encouragement of a non-Jew working in the sabbatical year, as he ruled ["Laws of the Sabbatical Year" 8:8] that "but to help [the non-Jew] physically is forbidden." It seems that [the rabbis] prohibited this to distance the Jew from agricultural work during the sabbatical year so that he would not then come to do work in his own field.[26] Therefore, if a Jew himself would sow the non-Jew's field during the sabbatical year, since he would be transgressing the words of the sages, it is right that he be prohibited [from being allowed to enjoy the produce] as a penalty.[27] According to this understanding, it would appear that the whole dispute between Maimonides and [other decisors] is only about issues on the level of rabbinic commandments.[28] However, concerning biblical commandments, Maimonides also thinks that so long as the land is in non-Jewish hands its holiness is suspended.

12. The prohibition of "Give them no foothold…"[29] in selling land to a non-Jew

Regarding the issue of "Give them no foothold [*lo teḥonem*]…,"[30] that it is prohibited to sell land to a non-Jew in the Land of Israel, one of the rabbinical court, the great Rabbi Z. Schach,[31] may his light shine,

29. Deut. 7:2.
30. Three separate laws are derived by the Talmud (Avoda Zara 20a) from the biblical words *lo teḥonem* – literally "you shall not be gracious" (i.e., to idolaters) (Deut. 7:2). One of these is that one may not give them a foothold in the land of Israel by selling them land. To the extent that this is interpreted as applying to non-Jews in contemporary times, it clearly poses a problem for the *heter mekhira* device, which is based on selling land in Israel temporarily to non-Jews. Rav Kook discusses the contemporary status of Islam and Christianity in *Mishpat Kohen,* responsum 58, p. 122, where he rules in line with the normative Jewish position that Islam is not considered to be idolatrous and inclines toward the view of Rabbi Menachem HaMeiri (1249–1315) that Christianity is also not idolatrous. These views on Islam and Christianity provide further reasons for leniency on the question of selling land to non-Jews in Israel, in addition to the arguments presented here.
31. Rabbi Zalman Schach (d. 1929), a judge on the Jaffa rabbinical court that Rav Kook headed.

התוספת, מה שמוסיפים עליה עתה, אסורה מן התורה; ויותר נכון לפי זה לבחור בגוי שכבר יש לו קרקע בארץ ישראל. אף על גב דיש לומר, שאם יקנה ממנו ישראל הקרקע הקודמת אז הלוא תצא החניה מתחת ידו, ונמצא אז שבקרקע זו הנמכרת לו כעת ניתנה לו חניה בקרקע, מכל מקום יש לומר דבתר השתא אזלינן, ועכשיו הוא אינו נותן לו חניה בקרקע, שהרי כבר יש לו מקודם, והוא מקושר לארץ ישראל בלאו הכי על ידי קרקע שיש לו מכבר...

ובכלל יש לומר, דנהי דלגבי איסור תורה יש מקום לומר, שאף על פי שעיקר המכירה אין עושין רק להפקיע איסורא, ולא שתישאר הקרקע באמת לנכרי, מכל מקום אין לנו לחלק מסברא לצאת מגזירת התורה, שכיוון שבכלל מכירה הוא הווי גם כן בכלל איסור, אבל באיסור דרבנן יש לומר דלא גזרו רק במקום ששייך עיקר האיסור באמת, כשמוכר ממש מכירה קיימת להעמיד ביד נכרי, אבל כשמוכר להפקיע איסורא לא גזרו כלל, ומכל שכן באיסור זה שעיקרו הוא משום תיקון יישוב ישראל בארץ ישראל ודאי צריך לומר דלא שייכא גזירה, דוגמת הא דאמרינן "הוא עצמו מחזר עליו לשרפו - מיכל קא אכיל מיניה" (פסחים י"א א').

32. I.e., in the shemitta year.

33. The important claim here is that in the case of a commandment forbidden from the Torah we do not take into account the reason for the commandment in considering the scope of its application; in the case of a rabbinical commandment, on the other hand, we do take into account the reason, and limit its application in case that would clearly undermine the underlying rationale.

34. The reference is to a discussion in the Talmud of whether one may search for *ḥametz* (leavened matter) on the eve of Pesaḥ after the time when eating *ḥametz* is allowed.

correctly commented, that one might say that in the case of a non-Jew who would anyway have a dwelling place [*ḥaniya*] in Israel [even without one's selling him more land], the addition – what one is adding [to his holding] now [through the sale] – is not prohibited by the Torah. According to this view, it is therefore preferable to choose [to sell to] a non-Jew who already owns land in the Land of Israel. Even though one could say that if a Jew were to buy his original piece of land, then the non-Jew's foothold in Israel would be removed, and the land that one would currently sell him would restore it to him; nevertheless, one could answer that we follow the current situation. Right now, [the sale of land] does not give [the non-Jew] a foothold in the land because he already has one; he is connected to the Land of Israel without [the current sale] through his original land holding....

In general, we may say that in the case of a biblical prohibition, even though the purpose of selling the land is to suspend the [sabbatical] restrictions against working the land[32] and the land will not ultimately remain in the non-Jew's hand; still, we do not make fine distinctions to get around a decree of the Torah because the act of selling is itself also forbidden. However, the rabbinic prohibition was instituted only [for cases] where the principle of the prohibition is actually relevant, that is, when it is a real sale and the land is to remain owned by the non-Jew. But when the sale is in order to suspend the prohibitions [against agricultural work], the rabbis did not legislate any objection at all.[33] What is more, when the purpose is in order to allow the settlement of Israel in the Land of Israel, it is certain that the [rabbinic] decree does not apply. The model for this is what is said (Pesaḥim 11a): "He himself seeks after the leavened bread [*ḥametz*] to burn it; will he then eat from it?"[34]

Rav Kook quotes the answer of Rava that since the point of the search is to destroy *ḥametz* that is found there is no concern that the searcher will eat any *ḥametz* he finds and the rabbis consequently saw no need to legislate in this case. Similarly, there is no need to legislate further rabbinic restrictions on selling land to a non-Jew in the case of the *heter mekhira* where the purpose is not to transfer the land permanently to non-Jewish ownership but to ease the restrictions of shemitta.

[יד]

שינוי המצב בין דורות הראשונים לדורות האחרונים – בהיתר המכירה

ומה שאנו סומכים על היתר השמיטה על ידי המכירה, ולא נמצא מעולם ולא נראה שסמכו על זה החכמים הקדמונים ז״ל, בזמן בית שני וכל ימי חכמי התלמוד הירושלמי והיישוב הנמשך בארץ ישראל אחר כך בימים הראשונים, אין זה פלא. ושלוש סיבות בדבר:

ראשונה, שמכיוון שהיו נוהגים אז איסור פירות שביעית גם בשל נכרים, משום גזירה אטו רוב קרקעות דשל ישראל (עיין בקונטרס אחרון לפ״ד הכ״ט בסה״ד), הלוא לא היה אפשר אז להתנהג באופן זה, מה שאין כן עכשיו, שכבר אין מניעה זו מפני שקרקעות של ישראל בארץ ישראל הם מיעוטא דמיעוטא, ודוחק המצב הלוא הוא גורם בהכרח להתנהג בהיתר של המכירה, מכיוון שיש מקום לסמוך על זה.

ושנית, ששנת השמיטה הלוא היתה אז קבועה וקיימת בזמנה שהיתה חלה בו, ולא נודע אז שום ספק ממניין השנים על שנת השמיטה – ועתה יש לצרף הספק של שנות השמיטה; שבא במחלוקת הרמב״ם והגאונים, וכבר זכר זה המבי״ט וכתב, שעל זאת אולי סמכו להקל בפירות של נכרי, דכיוון דשביעית בזמן הזה דרבנן הווי ספק דרבנן לקולא (והובאו דבריו במשנה למלך ה׳ מגילה פ״א הי״א)...

35. *Kuntrus Aharon* is a collection of detailed halakhic notes appended to the end of *Shabbat HaAretz*. Rav Kook suggests there that the principal reason for the rabbinic decree in ancient times against eating produce grown by non-Jews in Israel was to prevent people taking shemitta lightly and coming to eat food grown by Jews.

36. Exercising the *heter mekhira* would not have helped in this situation, as food grown on non-Jewish-owned land was forbidden.

37. See Maimonides, Laws of Shemitta (10:2–6) for a discussion and comparison of his opinion with that of the Geonim.

14. The changed situation between the earlier and later generations as regards the leniency to sell the land

Whereas today we rely on the leniency of selling the land during the sabbatical year, which has never been found [to have been used previously] and it does not seem that the earliest sages [*kadmonim*] of blessed memory relied on it during the Second Temple period, or in the era of the sages of the Jerusalem Talmud, or in the settlement in Israel that persisted afterwards during the days of the early sages [*rishonim*]. This is not surprising, and there are three reasons for it.

First, since in former times the custom was to forbid even produce grown by non-Jews during the sabbatical year because of the decree that one might come to eat from the majority of lands that were owned by Jews (see *Kuntrus Aḥaron* 84:2).[35] It was therefore not possible to act in this way.[36] Today, on the other hand, there is no such obstacle, because only a minority of a minority of the lands in Israel are owned by Jews. The necessity of the situation compels us to follow the leniency of selling the land, once there are grounds to rely on it.

Second, in those days, the sabbatical year was then fixed and fell at its proper time; there was no doubt then about the correct count of the years with respect to the sabbatical year. Today, however, there is doubt about when the sabbatical year occurs, which was a point of contention between Maimonides and the Geonim.[37] One may join this doubt together with the previous reason. Mabit already mentioned this issue,[38] writing that we may possibly rely on it as a ground for leniency to permit the produce of non-Jews. Since the sabbatical year in our time is of rabbinic authority, [we deploy the principle that] where there is a doubt over a rabbinic commandment, we may be lenient. (His view is cited in *Mishneh LeMelekh*,[39] "Laws of Megillah," 1:11.) ...

---

38. In Responsa of the Mabit, 1:21. I am grateful to Rabbi Benjamin Elton for identifying the source of this reference.
39. A classic commentary on Maimonides' *Mishneh Torah*, written by the eighteenth-century halakhist Rabbi Yehudah Rosenes.

ומלבד כל זה, עצם שינוי המנהג, שבדורות הראשונים, שאז לא היה גדול כל כך הצורך, לא נכנסו כל כך בהיתר הערמה ואחר כך בדורות האחרונים, כשנתגבר ההכרח, החלו להתיר בזה ולהנהיג כן את הציבור...

והיינו, שבכל מקום שלא היה ההכרח גדול לא רצו חכמי הדורות לפרסם היתר של הערמה, והווי בכלל "כבוד אלהים הסתר דבר" כהיתר של "מוליכו פחות פחות מד' אמות" במי שהחשיך לו בדרך (שבת קנ"ג ב'), ודבר זה היה מההוראות שאין מפרסמים אותן משום עמי הארץ, דלא לייתו למיסרך; וכהאי גוונא, דכי מורי רב לתלמידיה מורי להו כרבי מאיר וכי דריש בפירקא דריש כרבי יהודה (חולין ט"ו א'); וכן הא דאפילו לא קרא אדם אלא קריאת שמע שחרית וערבית קיים "לא ימוש", ודבר זה אסור לאמרו בפני עם הארץ (מנחות צ"ט ב'), שכשההכרח מחייב להנהיג כן מפני הדחק אז בוודאי מצווה להורות כן, בדברים אלו וכיוצא בזה, כדי להסיר המכשול מהנכשלים ולהרוויח את הדוחק הגדול של אותה שעה. ומשום הכי החלו גם כן גדולי הדורות להנהיג בפומבי את מכירת החמץ כפי הנהוג, מאחר שנתברכו עסקי התעשיות ובתי החרושת באפנים גדולים, שאי אפשר היה בהם בלא פרסום דרך המכירה. וכן גבי ענייננו: בימים הראשונים, כשמעמד היישוב היה בעיקרו של יסוד עבודת אדמה לאכילה, היה אפשר להנהיג קדושת שביעית כדת בלא היתר

40. Prov. 25:2; Rav Kook cites this verse to support the view that where there is no compelling societal need to publicize a halakhic leniency, it is preferable not to.

41. The case is of a traveler who finds himself still on the road on Friday evening when Shabbat begins. Can he continue to travel and safeguard his valuables since it is forbidden to carry in public places on Shabbat? The solution to his predicament which, the Talmud confides, "the sages did not wish to reveal," is that he may carry his belongings in increments of four cubits (about six feet) at a time, i.e., putting down and picking up his bundle every four cubits. Carrying less than four cubits is rabbinically forbidden, but the rabbis allowed the traveler to move his valuables in this way when no other option was available. The sages concealed this solution for fear that it would be misused by unscrupulous people not in the traveler's particular situation.

42. The case concerns a dispute between R. Meir and R. Yehuda about whether one may eat food that a Jew has inadvertently cooked on Shabbat. Privately Rav followed the lenient opinion of R. Meir that one may, but publicly he taught R. Yehuda's opinion lest people would abuse the lenient view (e.g., by cooking deliberately and then pretending to have done so inadvertently).

Apart from all this, the basic reason for the change in custom is that in the earlier generations, when the need was not so great, [the sages] did not involve themselves much with leniencies through legal fictions [*haarama*]. Afterward, in later generations, when the need increased, they began to permit through this [leniency] and to propound it publicly....

If there was no great necessity, the sages did not want to publicize a leniency based on a legal fiction. This falls under the rubric: "It is the glory of God to conceal a matter."[40] This is similar to the leniency of "he moves it less than four cubits," in the case of someone who is traveling when it becomes dark on Friday afternoon (Shabbat 153b).[41] This was one of those teachings that the rabbis did not publicize out of a concern that ignoramuses might misuse them. In similar fashion, "When Rav taught his students he would rule like R. Meir, but when he gave a public lecture, he ruled according to R. Yehuda's opinion" (Ḥullin 15a).[42] A further example: Even if a person merely recites the *Shema* during the morning and evening, he fulfills "Let not [this Book of the Teaching] cease [from your lips],"[43] but it is forbidden to say this in front of an ignoramus (Menaḥot 99b).[44] In all of these as well as other similar cases, when necessity requires us to act, due to distress, according to [such leniencies] then obviously it is a commandment to teach them, in order to remove stumbling blocks from before those who are prone to stumble and to relieve the great distress of that particular time. Therefore, even the great rabbis of the generation began to publicly teach that one may sell leavened bread [before Passover], as is our custom, when Jews were blessed with large businesses and factories that could not have survived without the publicization of [the leniency] to sell leavened bread.[45] So too with our subject: In former times when the [economic] status of Jewish settlement in Israel was based on working the land in order to subsist, it was possible to observe the sabbatical year according to the

43. Josh. 1:8.
44. The ignoramus, knowing that he could fulfill the mitzva of Torah study simply by saying the *Shema* prayer twice a day, might feel little incentive to invest further in learning Torah.
45. In the late medieval period when Jews became heavily involved in the beer business.

של הפקעה, שהרי סוף סוף היו הפירות מופקרים והיה על ידי זה ריווח לעניים והיה קרוב לכוונת התורה "ואכלו אביוני עמך" על כן לא נתפרסם אז היתר של הפקעה על ידי מכירה. אבל בימינו שיסוד היישוב הוא על ידי מסחר בפרי תבואות המושבות, וכשיימנע מהלך המסחר תיהרס גם כל פרנסתו ומעמדו על להבא – במצב כזה ודאי חובה להנהיג את היתר ההפקעה על ידי המכירה, על פי הסכמת חכמים בכל שמיטה, עד אשר ירחם ד׳ את עמו וארצו וישובו הימים הטובים, ויהיה אפשר גם מצד מהלך המסחר לשמור קדושת השביעית כדינה במילואה, בלא שום הפקעה.

[טו]

קדושת הארץ וקדושת המצוות

אמנם ידידי הגאון ר׳ יעקב דוד רידב"ז שליט"א, העיר בקונטרס השמיטה אשר לו: איך אפשר לומר, שנתיר להפקיע את מצוות שביעית על ידי הפקעת המכירה, משום שאנו אומרים שלגבי שביעית בזמן הזה יש קניין לנכרי להפקיע, משום יישוב ארץ ישראל – הרי כיוון שאנו מפקיעים אותה מקדושתה אין כאן מצוות יישוב ארץ ישראל.

אבל כל זה מיוסד רק על הסברא, שאין שום מעלה אחרת לארץ ישראל מלבד מה שעל ידה אפשר לקיים את המצוות התלויות בה, והיא לפי זה רק כעין הכשר להמצוות התלויות בארץ, לפיכך כשמפקיעים חובת המצוות, אפילו

46. Ex. 23:11.

47. In 1909, when *Shabbat HaAretz* was written, the nascent Jewish settlement had already begun exporting citrus fruits to Europe. Rav Kook implies here that exports markets lost during the shemitta year will not be easily recovered.

48. Rabbi Yaakov David Willowsky (1845–1913), chief rabbi of Safed and Rav Kook's leading opponent in the controversy over the *heter mekhira*.

law [*kedat*] without the leniency of [selling the land] to suspend [its sabbatical holiness], for, in any case, produce was rendered ownerless in the sabbatical year and the poor benefited, and it was close to the intention of the Torah: "[In the seventh (year) you shall let it rest and lie fallow.] Let the needy among your people eat of it."[46] Consequently, they did not publicize the leniency to suspend [the land's holiness] through sale [to a non-Jew]. However, in our times, when the settlement [of the Land of Israel] is based on trade of its agricultural produce, and preventing the flow of trade will also destroy its livelihood and economic viability in the future,[47] there is a clear obligation to follow the leniency of suspending [the land's holiness] through sale, with the sages' agreement each year, until God has mercy upon His people and His land, and brings back the good times so that it will be possible from an economic point of view as well to observe the holiness of the sabbatical year in the fullness of its laws, without any suspension.

15. The holiness of the Land of Israel and the holiness of the commandments

However, my friend the great scholar , Rabbi Yaakov David, the Ridbaz,[48] may he merit a long and good life, has made the following point in his book about the sabbatical year: How is it possible that we can suspend the commandment of the sabbatical year through selling [the land], because we argue that we can suspend the sabbatical year at this time by the acquisition of a non-Jew in order to settle the Land of Israel? Yet, since we uproot the holiness of the land, there is no longer a commandment to settle it![49]

However, this [question] is all based on the notion that the Land of Israel has no special value except for enabling us to fulfill the commandments that are dependent on the land. According to this, [the Land of Israel] is a kind of a preparation for the commandments dependent on the land. Therefore, when we suspend the obligation of the commandments,

49. Ridbaz argued that the concept underlying the *heter mekhira* is self-defeating; we suspend the holiness of the land in order to encourage settlement, which is predicated on the land's holiness!

על פי הכרח, שוב אין כאן מצוות יישוב ארץ ישראל. ובאמת לא כן הדבר; וסברא זו אינה מיוסדת על פי עיקר יסודה של תורה, התלויה ביסוד קדושתה העליונה גם היא בארץ ישראל, ו״מלכה ושריה בגוים אין תורה״ ״וכיוון שגלו ישראל ממקומם אין לך ביטול תורה גדול מזה״ (חגיגה ה׳ א׳). כי ארץ ישראל דומה בזה לתלמוד תורה: ותלמוד תורה, אף על פי שהוא מביא לידי מעשה המצוות כולן, מכל מקום חלילה לומר, שערכה של תורה איננו כי אם הכשר למעשה המצוות, אבל היא עליונה וחשובה בקדושתה בפני עצמה, עד שאפילו כשלומדין מה שאי אפשר לקיים כלל אין שיעור למעלת הלימוד ההוא, ועוד הוא גדול באיזה פנים מן הלימוד שאפשר לקיימו במעשה, שהרי זה נחשב גם כן עשייה, כדאמרינן (מנחות ק״י א׳): ״כל העוסק בתורת חטאת כאילו הקריב חטאת וכל העוסק בתורת אשם כאילו הקריב אשם״, ואין שיעור למעלת התורה של הלימוד בדברים שאין להם שום יחס לענייני מעשים, כי היא בעצמה עליונה מכל; אלא שבכלל גודל מעלתה כלולה גם מעלה זו שהיא מביאה לידי מעשה. כמו כן היא קדושת ארץ ישראל, אף על פי שבקדושתה היא מביאה אותנו גם בחורבנה לידי כמה מצוות, שאין לנו דוגמתן בחוץ לארץ, וקל וחומר בבניינה...

ואפילו אם מפני הדוחק צריכים להפקיע איזו מצווה מהמצוות התלויות בארץ לא ייפול על זה, חס ושלום, לבם של הזוכים להסתופף בצלצח קדושת חיבת נעימת ארץ חמדה אשר עיני ה׳ אלהינו בה תמיד, מראשית השנה עד אחרית שנה, ״מה ידידות משכנותיך ה׳ צבאות נכספה וגם כלתה נפשי לחצרות ד׳, לבי ובשרי ירננו אל אל חי״. כי עצם ישיבת ארץ ישראל מצד עצמה שקולה היא נגד כל המצוות שבתורה, שבכלל כל המצוות כלולות גם כל המצוות

50. Rav Kook responds to Ridbaz by distinguishing between a kind of holiness that obligates us to perform the land-dependent mitzvot, which can be suspended, and a higher inherent holiness to the land that endures, independent of sales under the *heter mekhira*.

51. Lam. 2:9; NJPS modified.

52. Living in the Land of Israel has an encompassing value for the Torah study that it makes possible.

53. Cf. Kiddushin 40b, where studying Torah is judged preferable to action because "Torah leads to action."

even due to necessity, there is no longer a commandment to settle the land. But this is not so. His premise has no foundation in the fundamental principle of the Torah [*ikar yesod haTorah*], which depends on the principle of the high holiness also of the Land of Israel:[50] "Her king and her leaders are in exile, Torah is no more."[51] And, "Since Israel has been exiled from its place, there is no greater neglect of Torah than this!" (Ḥagiga 5a).[52] The Land of Israel is like the study of Torah in this respect: Even though the study of Torah brings one to perform all of the commandments,[53] heaven forbid that one should say that the entire value of the study of Torah consists in preparing us to do the commandments. On the contrary, the study of Torah has its own exalted and overriding holiness to the point that even when we learn [about commandments] that we are unable to fulfill at all, the learning is still of the highest possible value. Indeed, there is a sense in which such study is even greater than study which can be fulfilled in action, as they said, "If one studies the Torah of sin offerings, it is as if he offered a sin offering; if one studies the Torah of a guilt offering, it is as if he offered a guilt offering" (Menaḥot 110a). There is no level higher than the study of subjects of the Torah that have no connection to practice; it is higher than everything. That said, the capacity of the study of Torah to lead to practice is a part of its greatness. The same is true of the holiness of the Land of Israel. Even though its holiness, despite its state of devastation, still enables us to fulfill certain commandments that we cannot perform outside of Israel, which will be all the truer when it is rebuilt....

Even if out of duress, one of the commandments that are dependent on the land has to be suspended, this would not, heaven forbid, break the spirit of those who are privileged to dwell... in this precious land, "on which the Lord your God always keeps His eye, from year's beginning to year's end";[54] "How lovely is Your dwelling-place, O Lord of hosts. I long, I yearn for the courts of the Lord; my body and soul shout for joy to the living God."[55] The very act of living in the Land of Israel is equal in weight to all of the commandments in the Torah,[56] within

---

54. Deut. 11:12.
55. Ps. 84:2–3.
56. Cf. Sifrei on *Parashat Re'eh*.

התלויות בארץ... שעיקר קדושתה של ארץ ישראל היא הישיבה בה בעצמה, וממילא נמשכות עם זה הזכויות של המצוות התלויות בארץ, אבל גם כשהן נפקעות על ידי דחק עומדת היא בעצם רוממות מעלת קדושתה, וצריך כל לב וכל רוח ונשמה של כל אחד ואחד מישראל להיות הומה ושוקק לבוא להיאחז בארץ חמדה, במקום בית חיי עם ד׳ לדור ודור ולנצח נצחים...

והרי היא בעצמה שקולה גם בפרטיותה כנגד כל מצוותיה של תורה, ואינה רק הכשר לקיום המצוות, וממילא אין לבוא שום רפיון ידיים, בחשק אהבתם של ישראל לארץ ישראל, אם מפני הכרח המצב הירוד של אחר החורבן, מפני נגישות הגויים או דוחק פרנסה, יוכרחו להפקיע חיוב איזו מהמצוות על ידי איזו תחבולה, המותרת בשעת הדחק על פי דין תורה, כהא דפרוזבול...

ואם כך היא המידה גם ביחס הפרט של כל יחיד ויחיד, שמחויב הוא בוודאי בכל כוחו ואונו להוציא מן הכוח אל הפועל את חיוב התשוקה, לבוא להיאחז בארץ ישראל, ולא ישקע את עצמו בארץ העמים, אשר "בגוים אין תורה" (ספרי פ׳ עקב) ו"דומה כמי שאין לו אלוה" ו"ישראל שבחוץ לארץ עובדי עבודה זרה בטהרה הם" – כמה כפולה ומכופלת היא לאין שיעור וערך המצווה הגדולה הזאת ביחס אל הכלל! על כן בכל עת אשר אנו רואים, שמתחילים ישראל לשום לבם לשוב לארץ ישראל, והם מוציאים לפועל את תשוקת לבבם זאת במכסת נפשות, עדה וקהל, אנו מכירים בזה יד ד׳ שהואיל לזכות את ישראל במצווה הגדולה הזאת, השקולה כנגד כל המצוות שבתורה מצד עצם עצמותה. ואם יזדמן, שעל ידי חיוב של איזו מהמצוות התלויות בארץ יכבד עניין הישיבה

57. See above, p. 96, note 14.
58. Sifrei, *Parashat Ekev*.

which the commandments that depend on the land are included.... This means that the principle of the holiness of the Land of Israel consists in living in it. The merit of being able to fulfill the commandments dependent on the land necessarily follows from living in the land, but if these commandments were suspended because of duress, the exalted holiness of the land itself would remain. The heart, spirit, and soul of every single member of Israel should yearn and desire to come and take hold of this precious land, the eternal home for the life of God's people....

[Living in the land] is, in itself, even in its details, considered to be equal to all of the commandments of the Torah, and it is not a mere enabling condition for the fulfillment of commandments. There should thus be no weakening in the passionate love of [the people of] Israel for the Land of Israel, if, out of necessity in our lowly situation following the destruction, either because of the impact of the gentiles or the exigencies of earning a living, we will be forced to suspend the obligation of certain commandments using some legal devices [*taḥbula*] that are permitted according to Torah law [*din Torah*] in times of need. [Examples include:] the *prozbul*....[57]

If it is true of every individual that he is certainly obligated to try with all his strength and might to bring his obligation of love of the land from potentiality to actuality and to come and take his share in it and not to settle permanently in the lands of the nations – where "there is no Torah among the nations,"[58] "he is like one who has no God,"[59] and "Israel outside the Land of Israel inadvertently worship idols"[60] – then how many more, innumerable times over is this true of this great commandment as it applies to the collective! Therefore, we see that in any era when Israel begins to turn their hearts toward a return to the Land of Israel, and they actualize this desire and clothe it in the actions of congregations and communities, then we recognize that Israel is being privileged to fulfill this great commandment, that in its essence is equal in weight to all of the commandments of the Torah. If it turns out that through the obligation to keep one of the commandments that are dependent on the land, settling the land becomes more difficult due to

59. Ketubot 110b.
60. Ibid.

בארץ, לפי המצב הדחוק והפרנסה המצומצמת – אשר כך היא המידה בתחילת התנוצצות אור גאולה וישועה, כדכתיב: "כי עם בציון ישב בירושלים בכו לא תבכה חנון יחנך לקול זעקך, כשמעתו ענך. ונתן לכם ד׳ לחם צר ומים לחץ ולא יכנף עוד מוריך, והיו עיניך רואות את מוריך" – באופן, שעל ידי מניעת ההפקעה של איזו מצווה או מניעת הוראה לקולא, במה שהוא אפשר על פי גדרי תורה, יבוא ביטול או עיכוב לעניין המצווה הגדולה והכללית של ישיבת ארץ ישראל – אז בוודאי חיובא רמיא על כל בעל הוראה, להיות עיניו ולבו תמיד בטובתם של ישראל, ולא לחוש כלל למה שמפקיעים לשעה איזו מצווה מפני ההכרח: כי סוף כל סוף ישיבת ארץ ישראל מצד עצמה היא שקולה כנגד כל המצוות. ולא עוד אלא, שהמשכתם של ישראל לבוא לארץ ישראל, היא הגורם היסודי לכל התשועות ולכל הקדושות...

אמנם בוודאי צדקו מאוד דברי הגאון בית הלוי ז״ל בתרעומתו נגד אותם, אשר באו לעקור המצווה בסברות שדופות קדים, בלא שום הפקעה ובלא שום הגדרה וחילוק בין מלאכות של תורה לשל דבריהם – כי אנו צריכים לעסוק בעניין קדוש זה, בכובד ראש ויראת ד׳, גדולה וטהורה, למען שמו הגדול ולמען עמו ונחלתו. וכן כמה חסדאין מיליה שם, שהאריך להראות, כמה גדולה היא מצוות שביעית וכיוצא בה מן המצוות התלויות בארץ, אפילו אם נפטרנו מהן מן התורה על ידי הפסק היובל, שמכל מקום הן בכלל אזהרת חז״ל בספרי (פ׳ עקב סמ״ג) שדרשוה על דברי ירמיה: "הציבי לך ציונים – היו מצוינים במצוות". והרבה עד אין קץ יש, ואנו חייבים בוודאי, להעיר ולעורר באהבת נועמן וגודל

61. Isa. 3:20.

62. Rabbi Yosef Dov Soloveitchik, 1820–92 (great grandfather of his namesake, the twentieth-century leader of American Modern Orthodoxy).

63. *Parashat Ekev*, sec. 43.

64. Jer. 31:20.

65. This midrash posits that the reason for the fulfillment of the commandments in the exile is for the purpose of "setting for yourself road markers," that is, to remember the commandments so that they not be forgotten and can be observed when we return to Israel; this idea was developed by Nahmanides in his Torah commentary

straitened circumstances and limited livelihoods – this being the case in the initial flickering of the light of redemption and salvation, as it says: "Indeed, O people in Zion, dwellers of Jerusalem, you shall not have cause to weep. He will grant you His favor at the sound of your cry; He will respond as soon as He hears it. My Lord will provide for you meager bread and scant water. Then your Guide will no more be ignored, but your eyes will watch your Guide."[61] So that for the want of suspending a certain commandment or for the lack of a lenient ruling, when it would possible within the bounds of the Torah, fulfillment of this great and encompassing commandment of settling the Land of Israel would be nullified or delayed, then there is certainly a heavy obligation incumbent upon every appropriate ruler [*baal horaa*] to always take to heart and to keep in view the good of Israel. He should not be concerned about temporarily suspending some commandment out of necessity, for ultimately the settlement of the Land of Israel is equal in weight to all of the commandments. Moreover, the continuation of Israel coming to the Land of Israel is the fundamental cause of all salvations and holy things....

However, the great scholar Beit Halevi[62] of blessed memory was quite justified in his polemic against those who come and uproot commandments with reasons that are flimsy as reeds, without any suspension, definitions, or distinctions between [agricultural] work [that is prohibited] by the Torah or by the rabbis. We must deal with this holy matter with level-headedness and great, pure fear of God for the sake of His great name, people, and inheritance. There are some devout words by which he elaborates on the greatness of the commandment of the sabbatical year and the other commandments that depend on the land, and [says] that even if we are exempt from them according to the Torah through the cessation of the Jubilee, nevertheless, they are included in the warning of the sages in the Sifrei,[63] who interpret the words of Jeremiah, "Erect markers [*hatzivi lakh tziyunim*],"[64] to mean "become distinguished [*metzuyanim*] before Me through commandments [*mitzvot*]."[65] It is certainly the case that we must awaken and rouse

---

to Lev. 18:25 and Deut. 11:18. The suggestion here is that even in Israel, not forgetting the mitzvot is an additional reason for their full observance wherever possible.

ערכן של המצוות בכלל ומצוות ארץ חמדתנו ובית חיינו בפרט, שהן מציבות אותנו להיות לעם לד׳ אלהינו, לחיותנו עדי עד. ואפילו מה שיש פנים להיפטר ממנו על ידי איזו תחבולה, גם כן נאה ויאה לעם קדוש שומר אמונים – ובפרט ליושבים בארץ ד׳ וחבל נחלתו – שיתמלאו באהבת ד׳ יתברך וחשק מצוותיו וישתדלו לקיים באהבה גם את זה. אבל מצד משקל אהבת השם יתברך, אהבת המצוות ואהבת הארץ וקדושתה המחוברת באהבת כללות האומה, עם בחר לו י־ה, ישראל לסגולתו, צריך העניין למשקל כחוק משקל החסידות, שעל זה נאמר ״ושם דרך אראנו בישע אלהים״, ומה שהמצב גורם ומכריח להקל ולהפקיע, אשר אי לאו הכי תתבטל או אפילו תתעכב התרחבות יישוב ארצנו הקדושה, חלילה לומר לבחור בזה במידת חסידות להחמיר, במקום שיש פנים להקל בפרטי המצוות, ולגרום על ידי חומרא זו קולא נוראה של ביטול ופחת מצוות ישיבת ארץ ישראל, השקולה כנגד כל המצוות, אל הכלל כולו...

וכמו שביארנו בקדושתה היא קיימת, לגבי כל המעלות וכל הברכות, האמורות לכלל ולפרט, וכל הקדושות העליונות הקשורות בארץ ישראל לעדי עד, בין כשהיא בידי ישראל ובין כשהיא מכורה לנכרים וחוץ ממה שההפקעה אינה אלא לשעה וקיום יישוב ארץ ישראל הוא לדורות, ועל ידי התחזקות יישוב ארץ ישראל תשובנה לנו כל החמודות הקדושות כולן וכל המצוות התלויות בארץ בכללן, ודמי ל״אמרה תורה חלל עליו שבת אחת כדי שישמור שבתות הרבה״ – חוץ מזה, גם מצד עצמה באותה השנה עצמה מתקיימת מצוות ישיבת

66. For a classic discussion of the issue of balancing stringent saintliness with the normative requirements of the commandments, see Rabbi Moshe Chaim Luzzato (1707–1746), *Path of the Just*, ch. 18.

67. Ps. 50:23.

68. The context of this citation, from Talmud Shabbat 151b, is: to save a live day-old baby, we may desecrate Shabbat; the Torah said, "profane one Shabbat for him, so that he will observe many Sabbaths." Rav Kook draws an analogy between this principle and his exhortation that where necessary farmers should employ the device of suspending observance of shemitta through the *heter mekhira*, so as to ensure the survival of

ourselves to the faithful love and great value of the commandments in general and those that relate to our treasured country and eternal homeland in particular, for they mold [*matziv*] us into God's people, giving us eternal life. Even if we could somehow exempt ourselves from them through some device, it would still be right and fitting for the holy nation that keeps the faith, especially those who dwell in the Lord's land and inheritance, to fill themselves with the love of God, may He be blessed, and with yearning for His commandments and to strive lovingly to fulfill even this [commandment]. However, from the perspective of balancing love of God, love of the commandments, love of the Land [of Israel], and its holiness, together with love of the whole people [*ha'uma*] – this requires a kind of balancing that is similar to the norm of weighing saintliness [in the performance of commandments],[66] about which it is said, "and to him who improves his way, I will show the salvation of God."[67] Far be it for anyone to say to us to choose stringent saintliness [*midat ḥasidut lehaḥmir*] concerning those [commandments] which the situation causes us to treat leniently [*lehakel*] and to suspend, since otherwise the expansion of settlement in our Holy Land would be neglected or even prevented, and [thus] to cause through this stringency the dreadful laxity of neglect and diminishment of the commandment of settling the Land of Israel, which is equal in weight to every and all commandments....

As we have explained, the land remains holy regarding all the exalted qualities and blessings that have been promised to the individual and the collective. All the high holinesses [are] connected to the Land of Israel forever and ever, when it is owned by a Jew or when it has been sold to non-Jews.... [This is] aside from the fact that the suspension [of the commandment] is only temporary, whereas the fulfillment of settlement of the Land of Israel will be for generations to come and through the strengthening of settlement in the Land of Israel all the holy, beloved things will be restored to us, as well as all of the commandments that are dependent on the land. [This is also] similar to [the rabbinic statement], "The Torah says: Desecrate one Shabbat so that one can observe many of them."[68] Apart from this, in [the sabbatical] year itself, the commandment

---

the vulnerable settlements and enable the observance of many more shemitta years in the future when the situation of Jewish settlement would be more secure.

ארץ ישראל, השקולה ככל המצוות שבתורה, בכל קדושתה והדר עליון השורה בתוכה – נמצא שיש מצווה להפקיע את המצווה לשעה, במקום הכרח, כדי לקיים את מצוות ישיבת ארץ ישראל, והמחמיר בזה יותר מן המידה, האפשרית להקל, אחר כל טורח ועמל העיון האפשרי בחדרי תורה, הריהו נוגע בנחלת ד׳, מונע צמיחת קרן ישועת ישראל ומבטל מישראל את המצווה העליונה והקדושה של ישיבת ארץ ישראל, השקולה ככל המצוות כולן.

ואין לנו ללכת כי אם בדרך ד׳, ״כאיש אשר אמו תנחמנו כן אנכי אנחמכם״, וצריכים אנו להשקיט לב היושבים והמתיישבים בארץ הקודש, שהם מוכרחים להשתמש בדרך היתר זה כפי המידה המוכרחת, להודיע אותם כי אשרי חלקם וכי טוב גורלם, שזכו לשבת בנחלת ד׳ ושהם שמים לב לקיום המצוות התלויות בארץ כפי כוחם, ומה שאי אפשר לקיימן הם מתנהגים בהן על פי דרכי הוראות חכמים להיפטר מחיובם עד עת רצון. וחלילה להוציא לעז על ישראל קדושים שבי ארץ שביה, המתנחלים על אדמת הקודש, השבים לביצרון ומייסדים יסוד מעלה ופתח תקווה וגאולה לבית ישראל, אשר באור ארץ חיים יאיר אופל גוי לא אלמן. ״ואתה אל תירא עבדי יעקב ואל תחת ישראל, כי הנני מושיעך מרחוק ואת זרעך – מארץ שבים, ושב יעקב ושקט ושאנן, ואין מחריד״...

---

69. I.e., of shemitta.

70. Isa. 66:13.

71. That is, until such a time when it would become economically possible to observe shemitta fully without relying on the *heter mekhira.*

72. In an elegant and surely intentional pair of puns, Rav Kook here alludes to two biblical phrases, that were used to name two of the earliest agricultural settlements of the First Aliyah: *Yesud Hamaala* ("foundation for a journey upwards," cf. Ezra 7:9) was the name of the first agricultural settlement in the Hula Valley, founded

of settling the Land of Israel will be fulfilled, which is equal in weight to all the commandments of the Torah, in all its holiness and exalted glory that dwells within it. It is therefore a commandment to suspend temporarily this commandment[69] in a time of need, in order to fulfill the commandment of settling the Land of Israel. One who is inappropriately strict in this matter, about which it is possible to be lenient, after all possible labor and toil in the [study] room of Torah, surely damages God's inheritance, stunts the flourishing of the horn of Israel's salvation, and deprives Israel of the exalted and holy commandment of settling the Land of Israel, which is equal to all the commandments.

We must only walk in the path of God. "As a mother comforts her son so I will comfort you."[70] We must calm the hearts of those who dwell in the Holy Land who are constrained to use this leniency according to the required measure. [We must] tell them how happy is their portion and how good is their lot, for they have merited to live in God's inheritance, they pay attention to fulfilling the commandments that depend on the Land [of Israel] according to their ability and, concerning what is impossible for them to fulfill, they act according to the teaching of the sages to exempt themselves from obligations until a more favorable time.[71] God forbid that anyone casts aspersions on holy Israel who return from the land of their captivity, who settle on the holy soil, who return to the fortress, who lay foundations for a journey upwards [*maala*] and an opening of hope [*petaḥ tikva*][72] and redemption for the house of Israel, who, through the light of the land of life, will illuminate the darkness of a nation that has not been left bereft.[73] "But you, have no fear, My servant Jacob, be not dismayed, O Israel! I will deliver you from far away, your folk from their land of captivity; and Jacob again shall have calm and quiet, with none to trouble him."[74]

---

in 1882, by religious immigrants from Romania; *Petach Tikva* ("Opening of Hope," cf. Hosea 2:15) founded in 1878, was the first agricultural settlement in the center of the country, today near to Tel Aviv. Rav Kook likely meant to reference both the physical settlements and the spiritual hopes that their names expressed.

73. The literal translation of the Hebrew is "a nation who has not been left a widower."

74. Jer. 46:27; the context is a prophecy of consolation promising the return of the Jewish people to the Land of Israel.

הנה אחרי כל האמור למעלה, אף על פי שיש פנים לכאן ולכאן במחלוקת הב"י והמבי"ט, אבל בשביל כך בוודאי לא ישוב חיוב שביעית בשדה של נכרי שהיא מופקעת, כדאמרינן שיש קניין לנכרי להפקיע מידי שביעית בשביעית בזמן הזה, כמו שזוהי דעת כל רבוותא קמאי הנ"ל. והב"י נוטה לומר שגם דעת הרמב"ם כך היא; ואף על פי שיותר נראה לומר שהרמב"ם לא נחית לכך, מכל מקום כדאי הם הגדולים שמנינו לסמוך עליהם בשעת הדחק, במה שהרבים סוברים שהוא דרבנן. ויש גם מי שאומרים שהיא רק מידת חסידות דעלמא בזמן הזה. מצורף לזה מה שיש סברת ארנונא, שעוד אין הדבר ברור שאין לסמוך על זה להתיר את כל העבודה של כל השדה, כדעת הלכות ארץ ישראל. ונוסף מה שישנם ספקות במניין שנת השביעית. והיתר שמתירים בעבודות שהן בעצמן דאורייתא אינו אלא על ידי נכרים... ובפרט, שאחרי המכירה אין כאן אפילו שבות, שהרי הכל מודים שסומכים על מכירות כאלה במילי דרבנן, וכיוון שאין הקרקע של ישראל, אפילו אם נאמר שלא נפקעה קדושתה, אין כאן שבות עליו במה שהגוי עובד בקרקע השייכת לגוי. ומה שעושים על ידי ישראל היינו רק מלאכות דרבנן, במקום הדחק כשאי אפשר באופן אחר. ובדבר איסור הסחורה והביעור וההוצאה לחוץ לארץ, כל מה דאפשר ודאי צריך לאהדורי אחרי כל דרכי ההיתר האמורים...

---

75. See above notes 19–20.

76. The opinion of Maimonides, the most important medieval authority, on the crucial question of whether shemitta in post-exilic times is based on Torah or rabbinic authority, is ambiguous and subject to considerable debate – part of which is summarized as follows by Arye Edrei of Tel Aviv University in an essential article about the *heter mekhira* controversy: "'...And the sabbatical year and the cancellation of loans is in any case rabbinic, as we have explained' (*Hil. Shemitta VeYovel* 10:9). Rabbi Karo interpreted that only the cancellation of loans is rabbinic, but that the sabbatical year is a biblical law. This interpretation of Maimonides' words is difficult since it assumes that R. Yehuda HaNasi, who established that the sabbatical year in our times is rabbinic (Moed Katan 2b; Gittin. 36a–b), was speaking only about the cancellation of loans, and not the cessation of work on the land ... this law appears as follows in manuscripts of Maimonides: 'And the sabbatical year in Israel is rabbinic and so too, the cancellation of loans is in any case rabbinic, as we have explained.'" See Yitzhak Shilat, *Rambam HaMeduyak* (Maaleh Adumim: Maaliyot Publishers, 2004), who comments that the word *midivreihem* (rabbinic) appears twice in that

After everything that has been said above, even though there are good arguments on both sides in the debate between Mabit and *Beit Yosef*,[75] this is certainly not sufficient to restore the obligation of the sabbatical year on land that is owned by a non-Jew, [an obligation] which has been suspended, because, as we have said, the purchase of land by a non-Jew does suspend the obligations of the sabbatical year during the sabbatical year in our times. This is the opinion of most of the early authorities, as we have seen. *Beit Yosef* inclines to the view that this is also Maimonides' opinion.[76] Even though it seems more likely that this was not Maimonides' view, the great rabbis that we have enumerated are enough to rely upon in a time of need, since many of them think that [the sabbatical year in these days] is of rabbinic authority. There are also those who think that in our times it is merely an act of piety.[77] Add to this the argument about taxes. [Add to this] as well the fact that there are doubts about the count of the sabbatical year. [Add to this as well] that the leniency that we propose [only allows] non-Jews [to perform agricultural work prohibited to Jews by the Torah].... In particular, after the sale there isn't even an additional rabbinic prohibition, for everyone agrees that we rely on such sales concerning rabbinic [regulations]. Since the land is not owned by a Jew, even if one claims that its holiness is not suspended, there is no additional rabbinic prohibition for the non-Jew works on land owned by a non-Jew. Jews will only perform [agricultural work] that is prohibited by rabbinic authority when it cannot be done in any other way....

law and was therefore omitted by the publisher. See Edrei, "From Orthodoxy to Religious Zionism: Rabbi Kook and the Sabbatical Year Polemic," note 35, available at: http://www.law.tau.ac.il/Heb/_Uploads/dbsAttachedFiles/22Edrei.pdf.

77. In addition to the two major opinions that Rav Kook has cited throughout his book, that shemitta in our times is in force either based on Torah authority or on rabbinic authority, there is a third opinion found among the Provence school of medieval commentators, that shemitta observance in post-exilic times is not mandatory at all and is only *midat ḥasidut* – an act of piety. This is the view of the Ravad (Rabbi Avraham ben David of Posquieres, c. 1125–98) and the Razah (Rabbi Zerachiah Halevi, "Baal HaMaor," c. 1115–85; Razah's view is quoted in *Sefer HaTerumot*, 55:4). The existence of this minority view constitutes for Rav Kook further grounds for leniency.

אחרי כל אלה אין מקום לערער על דרך הוראה כזו, במקום דחק שנוגע להפסד של רבים, אפילו אם לא היה הדבר נוגע לישיבת ארץ ישראל. וקל וחומר שהדבר נוגע ליסוד חיי נפש של ישיבת ארץ ישראל, ולא נקבעה בזה שום הלכה קבועה, רק בתור הוראת שעה: כשיתברר הדבר לבית דין הגון, הבקי במצב היישוב ובסדריו שאין דרך אחרת לקיומו של היישוב – יעשה את מעשיו לשם שמים, וד' עמו.

Given all of the above, there is no room to object to this way of ruling, in a situation of need that is connected to serious loss for the public, even if the matter did not have to do with settling the Land of Israel. How much more is this true when the question affects the very basis of the livelihoods for those who live in the Land of Israel, and also when it is not being fixed as a permanent law, but only as a temporary ruling. When the situation will be clarified to any fit rabbinical court, which understands the situation and the organization of the settlement in Israel [*yishuv*], that there is no other way to maintain this settlement, it will do this for the sake of heaven and God will be with it.

The Impact and Aftermath of *Shabbat HaAretz*

Shabbat HaAretz was the most detailed and systematic argument ever published in support of the *heter mekhira* and had the effect of institutionalizing the practice. After Rav Kook became the first chief rabbi of Palestine (in 1921), the chief rabbinate began to organize the shemitta-year sale of the land for the whole community and continued to do so after the foundation of the State of Israel in 1948.

The anti-*heter mekhira* ranks were strengthened in 1933, when Rabbi Avraham Yeshaya Karelitz (1878–1953), known by the name of his great halakhic work, the Ḥazon Ish, immigrated to Israel in 1933 (with Rav Kook's assistance) and became the unofficial leader of the Ḥaredi community there. The Ḥazon Ish was renowned for his immense learning, saintly character, and skepticism toward Zionism and the State of Israel. On the eve of the 1937–38 shemitta, he wrote a lengthy critique of Rav Kook's arguments in *Shabbat HaAretz* (after the latter's death).[1]

1. Despite their deep substantive disagreements, the Ḥazon Ish and Rav Kook held one another in high esteem. A well-known story relates how when Rav Kook came to Bnei Brak in 1934 for the foundation stone laying of the Novardok yeshiva, the Ḥazon Ish remained standing for the whole of the former's speech. *Moadei HaRe'aya*, ed. Moshe Zvi Neriyah (Jerusalem, 1980), 217–18.

The Ḥazon Ish believed that the Torah prohibition of selling land in Israel to non-Jews (Deut. 7:1–2) was an insurmountable obstacle to the *heter mekhira*. He argued against the notion that selling the land to non-Jews, even if permissible, could suspend its sanctity. While agreeing with Rav Kook that shemitta in our times is of rabbinic authority,[2] the Ḥazon Ish deployed this position against the *heter mehkira*, arguing that the Torah prohibition against selling the land couldn't be set aside to aid the rabbinically mandated observance of shemitta. Most fundamentally, the Ḥazon Ish rejected Rav Kook's meta-halakhic arguments that since the future of Jewish settlement in Israel was at stake, the halakha needed to be lenient. According to the Ḥazon Ish, "All of the murmurings that this is a situation of danger that demands lifesaving measures derives only from coldheartedness and a lack of the respect due to the performance of the Torah and its precepts."[3] The Ḥazon Ish denied Rav Kook's core premise that it was not feasible to observe shemitta in Israel. His constituency consisted not of the whole nation but of God-fearing farmers who were willing to sacrifice for the sake of the mitzvot; if they could observe shemitta properly and survive, that was sufficient for the Ḥazon Ish to demonstrate that shemitta observance was feasible.

The battle lines were drawn; Rav Kook implemented the *heter* for the whole Yishuv when he served as chief rabbi during the shemitta years of 1923–24 and 1930–31. On the other side, the Ḥazon Ish's position on *heter mekhira* is the Ḥaredi position until today. During the shemitta, his followers eat produce that is imported, grown by Arabs, or they rely on the *otzar beit din* method.[4] Most Religious Zionist Jews rely on the *heter mekhira*. Most secular and traditional Jews do, too, without caring much either way, because the official Israeli chief rabbinate (the

2. Ḥazon Ish, *Shevi'it* 3:7.
3. *Iggerot Ḥazon Ish* (Collection of the letters of the Ḥazon Ish) (Hebrew) (Bnei Brak: Greineman, 1990), 3:85.
4. *Otzar beit din* permits a court to hire agents to harvest produce in the normal way and then distribute it, for a fee, among the entire community. Similarly, a court is permitted to hire agents to press grapes for wine. This works because the court is not acting as an owner; the court has no proprietary rights in the field, and so the fundamental idea of shemitta, renunciation of ownership, is preserved.

Rabbanut) follows the *heter mekhira*, which is the official position of the Israeli government.

Until the shemitta of 2007–8, the Rabbanut gave its kosher certification to all *heter mekhira* produce – indeed, it performed the sale on behalf of interested farmers. In 2007, however, the Ḥaredi Rabbi Yonah Metzger was head of the Rabbanut; he announced that any Rabbanut-employed city rabbi who did not support the *heter* was allowed to revoke the kosher certification of any restaurants and hotels in his city that bought *heter mekhira* produce.

Rabbi Metzger created an absurd situation in which the body that implemented the *heter* could also refuse to recognize it. As non-*heter mekhira* produce is more expensive, this ruling could have spelled financial disaster for many. The Tzohar group of Religious Zionist rabbis announced that they would flout the chief rabbinate and issue *heter mekhira* certificates in cities where the local rabbis would not. Rabbi Rafi Feuerstein, chairman of Tzohar, said: "We believe that it is important to strengthen Jewish farmers and provide reasonably priced produce to the Jewish nation." Rabbi David Stav of Tzohar said: "We are trying to save the chief rabbinate from itself."[5]

Israel's supreme court intervened, ruling in October 2007 that the Rabbanut may not revoke the *heter mekhira* without a public process allowing farmers and others affected to be heard. Such a radical change of a century-old policy could not take place by fiat, the court declared. The *New York Times* covered the story, reporting that "rabbis are pitted against one another, the state and the religious authorities are in conflict, the Israeli Supreme Court is involved, the devout are confused and the cost of produce is rising."[6] I was interviewed on NPR about the controversy, doing my best to put a sympathetic gloss on these shenanigans. (The interviewer was, I recall, amused by the irony of Israeli religious Jews importing large amounts of food from Gaza during shemitta, at the same time as its Hamas rulers were raining missiles on Israel.)[7]

---

5. Quoted in Steven Erlanger, "As Farmers and Fields Rest, a Land Grows Restless," *New York Times*, October 8, 2007.
6. Ibid.
7. The interview is available at www.npr.org, "An Update on the Shmita Year."

Bafflement and anger reigned, and rabbis were ridiculed. The episode was further proof, if any was required, that the chief rabbinate was Rav Kook's least successful creation. In a painful historical irony, the chief rabbinate that Rav Kook built undermined the *heter mekhira* that he did more than anyone to promote.

SHEMITTA: 2014–15 AND BEYOND

Shabbat HaAretz instituted a paradoxical status quo that persisted for a century, whereby shemitta was observed in Israel primarily by avoiding its observance. Rav Kook compounded the paradox by publishing the halakhic argument of *Shabbat HaAretz*, which legitimated effectively avoiding the observance of shemitta, together with a non-halakhic introduction that elucidated the extraordinary potential socioeconomic and spiritual significance of shemitta when fully observed. This introduction was widely studied in Israel, sharpening the dissonance between what shemitta actually became and what Rav Kook had envisaged it might be.

The status quo of shemitta observance/nonobservance in Israel that has endured for one hundred years, since the publication of *Shabbat HaAretz*, is now crumbling. It is being eroded from two opposite sides. On the one hand, longstanding Ḥaredi opposition to the *heter mekhira* was expressed by the Rabbanut's declarations in 2007 and 2014 of its intention to withdraw support for the *heter*. On the other hand, a wave of grassroots initiatives comprising environmentalists, economists, social activists, and innovative religious thinkers, crossing communal-denominational lines and inspired partly by the 2011 social justice protests, is looking for ways to actively observe shemitta rather than avoid its observance. These initiatives seek to actualize the powerful teachings and values that they find in shemitta, relating to sustainable agriculture, debt relief, the economic commons, social justice, and much more, in the complex socioeconomic reality of twenty-first-century Israel.

The shemitta year of 2014–15 was a watershed in shemitta observance, with the institutional status quo coming under unprecedented pressure and, simultaneously, a plethora of innovative, grassroots-led, religiously meaningful and socioeconomically significant ways of actualizing the values of shemitta starting to emerge. Projects in Israel and the U.S. connected shemitta to debt forgiveness, social justice, and sustainable agriculture. A veteran of the Israeli technology sector, Yossi Tsuria, developed a list of forty-nine ways to enact the values of shemitta in the hi-tech sector.[8] The Israeli government sponsored significant shemitta initiatives spanning debt relief, education, and environmental conservation. Projects pioneered by SOVA, Hazon, Teva Ivri, and others aimed to show how shemitta addresses core, seemingly intractable, socioeconomic challenges that we all face: the growing polarization of wealth and poverty, our ceaseless exploitation of human and natural capital, and our very limited inability to predict, regulate, and moderate the periodic cyclical crashes to which the economy seems prone.

An extraordinary event held at the Knesset on January 6, 2014, showcased how different the coming shemitta would be. Knesset members and ministers spanning the political spectrum, left and right, religious and secular, spoke in support of measures to publicly implement broad values of shemitta in Israeli government policy. Several declared that the shameful politicking and public ridicule of the rabbinate in the last cycle had spurred them to want to restore the dignity of shemitta by enacting its real values. The leader of the opposition, Isaac Herzog (grandson of Rav Yitzhak Herzog, who succeeded Rav Kook as Ashkenazi chief rabbi), spoke passionately about the rich resources in Jewish tradition for renewing socioeconomic thought, shemitta foremost among them; Ruth Calderon, a Talmud educator who became a Knesset member (and who sponsored the gathering), declared the potential of shemitta to unite different factions of Israel society.

The government's chief economic adviser, Professor Eugene Kandel (a secular Russian immigrant to Israel), delivered a lecture on moral hazard and the *prozbul*; the education minister, Shai Piron, spoke about how all Israel's schoolchildren would learn about the socioeconomic and environmental values of shemitta in the coming year; the environment minister, Amir Peretz, announced measures to fund a moratorium on fishing in the Sea of Galilee during the shemitta year. Stocks had been almost exhausted by overfishing, but a year of respite would restore them to previous levels. Peretz also announced plans to open Israel's

8. For a summary, see http://blogs.timesofisrael.com/shmittah-in-hi-tech/.

national parks free of charge in the shemitta year, enacting the idea of the commons, while the Ministry of Welfare unveiled a planned fund of 70 million shekels to enable ten thousand Israelis to escape crushing debt this shemitta, in a joint initiative with major banks, utilities, and NGOs. Rabbi Yoel Bin Nun, a veteran Religious Zionist rabbi, shook his head and declared that all this energy, activity, and cross-party cooperation around the issue of shemitta was nothing short of miraculous.

Knesset member Shuli Mualem of the Jewish Home Party projected onto a screen passages from this book – the introduction to Rav Kook's *Shabbat HaAretz* – and studied them together with her Knesset colleagues and the assembled public. Her choice of the introduction to *Shabbat HaAretz* as a prism through which to view the fluid yet highly creative reality of the 2014–15 shemitta, testified to the book's enduring currency. Indeed, one way to understand the significance of the 2014–15 shemitta year was as slippage in the unstable relationship between the halakhic and aggadic parts of *Shabbat HaAretz*. The halakhic piece – the *heter mekhira* as a necessary device in a provisional reality – came under growing attack, while the aggadic vision of the book's introduction, of how shemitta might ideally be observed, began at last to blossom.

Seven Thoughts on the Present and Future of Shemitta

1. THE EFFECTS OF SHEMITTA OBSERVANCE ARE CUMULATIVE

> *This once-every-seven-years illumination carries an afterglow of divine ideals that will gradually shape our ethical characters so that the outlook that flows from them will become a deeper and more formative part of us.*

In Rav Kook's vision of a renewed shemitta, the insights and ethical achievements of each shemitta year build on one another. They influence the ensuing six years and become a baseline for the next cycle. Over successive seven-year cycles, new insights and expressions of shemitta emerge and grow organically out of previous iterations, in ways that cannot be predicted.

In this spirit, and anticipating the 2021–22 shemitta year, I conclude with a few remarks, that are neither exhaustive nor programmatic, based on observations about shemitta from the 2014–21 cycle. Each is paired with a quotation from the introduction to *Shabbat HaAretz*.

This is not to suggest that Rav Kook foresaw all these developments, but rather to acknowledge the enduring inspiration of his vision for a renewal of shemitta. These notes intentionally lead from the particularly Jewish toward the more universal. My hope is that they may help serve as a marker of where we have reached and be suggestive of directions in which shemitta observance[1] might develop in the future.

2. LEARNING LEADS TO ACTION

> *Studying the halakhot to gain clarity and breadth of understanding, writing books, and expanding research, all increase awareness and love of the mitzvot connected to the land, which were forgotten by most of the people for many centuries.*

At the rebirth of Jewish life in the Land of Israel, the renewal of shemitta required, first and foremost, a formidable effort of education. After some 1,800 years in which shemitta had been of virtually no practical relevance, a thorough reacquaintance with the laws and ideas of shemitta was essential for its observance to take root once again. Rav Kook strove to meet this need through a prodigious output of responsa, letters, lectures, and of course, writing and publishing *Shabbat HaAretz*. The talmudic quotation he cites, "learning leads to action," from Kiddushin 40b suggests an implicit acknowledgment of how prolonged the period of education could be. For among its proofs for the statement that learning leads to action, the Talmud observes that the giving of the Torah preceded the first shemitta by sixty-one years.[2] In choosing this source, Rav Kook hints that the initiation or renewal of shemitta might take some considerable time.

1. By "shemitta observance" I mean not just the halakhic requirements of shemitta as codified in works of Jewish law, but also the acts and values to which shemitta can inspire us.
2. Rashi, Kiddushin 40b, s.v. *Gadol Talmud*, explains the calculation of this number: after forty years of wandering the desert, it took a further fourteen years after entering the land for each farmer to become familiar with his land, and then an additional seven years until the first shemitta was observed.

Education was the cornerstone of the resurgence of interest in shemitta in Israel and beyond over the past two cycles. The germination period was lengthy, with the first modern article to consider social and environmental dimensions of shemitta appearing in 1966.[3] In the United States and Israel writings and teachings by, among others, Jeremy Benstein, Michael Melchior, Aharon Ariel Lavi, Arthur Waskow, and Yigal Deutscher, explored broader contemporary implications of shemitta. During the 2014–15 shemitta year in the United States, hundreds of schools and synagogues informally studied the subject, including many non-Orthodox institutions for whom shemitta had previously been obscure and irrelevant.

In Israel, there was a plethora of educational programs, study days, and symposia about the meanings of shemitta going far beyond the traditional preoccupation with whether or not to hold by the *heter*. The indefatigable shemitta activist, Einat Kramer, bought a large tent and traveled with it across the country, offering fruit shakes to thousands of passersby over the course of the year and engaging them in conversations about how the ideas of shemitta might apply today. This led to Kramer giving a series of weekly five- to ten-minute TV spots on the modern meanings of shemitta. "It [shemitta] became a conversation," said Kramer. "Until then there was never a conversation in Israel about it."[4]

The flourishing of interest in shemitta leading up to 2014–15 in the United States, was also remarkable. While the biblical shemitta of lands applies only in Israel, the concept began to resonate far beyond its borders.[5] The U.S. Jewish environmental movement adopted shemitta as a prescription against unsustainable agricultural practices, unabated

3. Blidstein, "Man and Nature in the Sabbatical Year," 50.
4. Quoted in David Krantz, "Shmita Revolution: The Reclamation and Reinvention of the Sabbatical Year," *Religions* 7 (2016): 21.
5. Remission of debts, *shemittat kesafim*, however, applies today on rabbinic authority, both inside and outside Israel: "*Shemittat kesafim* is practiced today on rabbinic authority, everywhere... so that the remission of debts not be forgotten in Israel" (Maimonides, *Mishneh Torah, Hilkhot Shemitta VeYovel* 9:3). In a brilliant analysis of the classic rabbinical sources, Rav Shagar notes how *shemittat kesafim* is both linked to the mitzvot that are dependent on the Land of Israel and also transcends them. Shimon Gershon Rosenberg (Shagar), *Gemara Shiurim: Shemitta* (Hebrew) (Alon Shevut, 2014), 55–59.

growth, and the alienation between people and their food and the earth. From 2007, Hazon, the largest Jewish environmental organization in the U.S., made shemitta a centerpiece of their educational programs. Hazon's founder, Nigel Savage, stresses the importance and centrality of the issues shemitta raises: "How do we relate to time? What's the balance between work and rest? ...How much is enough? ...What's the proper role of debt in a healthy society and how do we ensure the availability of credit?"

A series of meetings about shemitta between scholars and activists from Israel and the Diaspora led to an interesting cross-pollination of initiatives. One notable such event took place in London in June 2014 and concluded with a public discussion about shemitta between Daniel Taub, then Israel's Ambassador to the U.K., and Canon Giles Fraser, a prominent Church of England cleric. At the end of the dialogue, Fraser, whose father and two sons are Jewish, turned to Taub, as a representative of the State of Israel, and implored him, "Show us what it would look like to take this biblical wisdom and adapt it to a twenty-first-century economy. Please, show us what it would look like." Fraser's impassioned plea struck me both as a recognition that shemitta is a hallmark of ideal Jewish life[6] and also an intuition that its full realization will have universal interest.[7]

3. SHEMITTA OF WHAT?

A spirit of generosity will rest on all; God will bless the fruit of the land.

Arguably, the fundamental idea of shemitta is "the earth is Mine" (Lev. 25:23); the land belongs to God and not to people.[8] Land is a blessing

6. As noted in footnote 1 to the introduction to *Shabbat HaAretz*, above, Rav Kook saw the observance of shemitta as necessary for the full manifestation of the Jewish people's unique life on its land
7. Giles Fraser wrote about shemitta in his *Guardian* column ("Can Israel Really Decommission Its Agriculture Every Seven Years?" April 4, 2014). Fraser's recent memoir, *Chosen: Lost and Found between Judaism and Christianity* (Penguin, 2021), describes his journey to rediscover his Jewish family and religious roots.
8. Rabbi Yosef Zvi Rimon surveys the main reasons given for shemitta in traditional

held in trust, to be used for God's purposes. This means, above all, by stopping work, acknowledging the contingency of our possessions, and sharing them with the needy.

Creative, contemporary applications of shemitta implicitly or explicitly reckon with the question, what is the source of our wealth? When land was the main factor of production, observing the agricultural shemitta laws was a testing and transformative renunciation of control over the very source of life's blessings. Today when, in Israel, only 1.8 percent of the population works on the land, traditional shemitta observance does not touch the basis of most people's wealth. What then is the resource to which contemporary interpretations of shemitta should apply?

One response is to affirm that land is still the fundamental source of our well-being, and to note how we are apt to forget this. Few of us work in agriculture, but we all eat food, and so are dependent on the land. Shemitta, then, is an opportunity to restore our connection to land and renew awareness of how it sustains us. Rabbi Yaakov Ariel, a leading Religious Zionist rabbi in Israel, laments the thanklessness and poor compensation of farming, and the obliviousness of most of us to the struggles of those who produce our food. He urges that in the shemitta year city-dwellers take practical steps to show their indebtedness to the land and the farmers.[9] Rabbi Ariel thus connects halakhic observance of shemitta in Israel with the meta-halakhic value of appreciation for the land and those who work it.

In the U.S., Jewish environmentalists have interpreted shemitta as a call to reconnect to land through promoting more sustainable approaches to agriculture, encouraging local production, and stressing land as a community possession. Yigal Deutscher, an advocate of this approach, encourages us to "return food production to your own backyard and community commons. Share in the efforts of planting and

sources and argues that they all flow from this principle (Rimon, *Shemita: From the Sources to the Practical Halakha*, 25).

9. Specifically, Rabbi Ariel recommends that those who can afford to, buy more expensive *otzar beit din* (see explanation above) produce during the shemitta year. The source is a *shiur* I heard Rabbi Ariel give on May 3, 2021.

harvesting. Support community farms. Save seeds. Plant fruit trees.... Support respectful, healthy animal husbandry."[10]

A complementary answer to the question "Shemitta of what?" was suggested by Rabbi Yosef Zvi Rimon, author of a comprehensive guide to observing the laws of shemitta. Rabbi Rimon was also exercised by the challenge of how to make shemitta more meaningful in a hi-tech-based economy. Rabbi Rimon suggested that today time is our fundamental resource for producing value and that in shemitta we can "make a part of our time ownerless," and use it to help others.[11] Anyone can volunteer, and professionals whose time is valued highly can donate their services *pro bono*. In the 2014–15 shemitta year, Rabbi Rimon gave practical expression to this insight by establishing the highly successful "Hour of Shemitta" project in Israel – an online volunteering time bank that aimed to generate as many volunteer hours as there were hours in the shemitta year.

The shemitta in hi-tech initiative posited that whereas the main source of wealth in the Bible was land, today it is knowledge. As the digital revolution dematerializes the economy, innovative technology empowers its creators to capture vast markets. This trend only accelerated during the corona pandemic when digital solutions enabled us to work around the limits placed on face-to-face contact, movement, and commerce. Concentration of knowledge in a small sector of the population leads to great inequalities of wealth and power.

The question of how to make the values of shemitta real in an economy that is no longer agrarian but is driven by high-tech bothered me in the run-up to the 2014–15 shemitta year. As vice president of a solar energy company, the closest I came each day to getting dirt underneath my fingernails was when my turn came around to dump out the black gunk that accumulated in the filter of the coffee machine.

A group of tech executives led by Yossi Tzuria, co-founder of digital TV security pioneers NDS, was exercised by the same challenge

10. Yigal Deutscher, Tikkun Daily, "Embracing the Shemitta Cycle: A New Year Vision," Sep. 16, 2012 (see www.hazon.org/embracing-the-shmita-cycle-a-new-year-vision/).
11. Rimon, *Shemita: From the Sources to the Practical Halakha*, 27. Rabbi Dov Berkovits argues that energy is the fundamental input to modern economies and should be the main object of efforts to apply shemitta in contemporary conditions.

and developed a list of forty-nine ways to make shemitta real in Israeli high-tech. Tzuria's work was a creative yet authentic attempt to translate values of shemitta into the high-tech context. The word *shemitta* means letting go. Could we let go a little of things that we hold on to very tightly as exclusively ours, he wondered, and share them more widely? What if companies would donate to a "patent pool" patents of inventions that were not part of their core business and anyone anywhere in the world could use them on an open-source basis? Might companies allow low-price or even free distribution of some of their output during the shemitta enabling poorer consumers to experience products that they could not otherwise afford?

Or take the core shemitta value of renewal. In the seventh year farmers got to take a year off from working the land and devoted the time to rest, regeneration, and studying Torah. It is impossible to shut down the high-tech economy one year out of every seven. But, Tzuria wondered, could we find ways nonetheless to enact this value in ways that would benefit everyone by catalyzing a renewal of inventiveness and creativity? What about free classes in your company enabling staff to learn about the latest science in their field – or any other field? What if the company email stopped working outside normal business hours, so that emails sent at 2 a.m. would bounce back with an auto-message about work-life balance?

Inspired by this initiative, our solar company took some small steps to mark shemitta. We chose three measures. First, the company set a goal of cutting paper use by 50 percent during the shemitta year. This was fulfilled. Second, we attempted to outlaw the sending of work emails after 7 p.m. in the evening. The effort lasted for about a week. The norm of 24/7 availability in the hi-tech world (or 24/6 in our company, where most of the staff were Shabbat observant,) was too engrained. It would have needed a deep change in management mindset to break this pattern, even for a year. Third, we set up a weekly series of shemitta talks. Every week, a different team member gave a talk to the rest of the company about anything of interest to them, from the intern who presented a slideshow on his post-army trip to South America, to the CEO who spoke about his student activism for Soviet Jewry. This simple innovation had a surprising effect on the company culture. We learned about unknown sides of colleagues whom we worked with every day. It went a little way toward softening the hierarchies in the company and acquainting us with the wholeness of each other's lives.

I know of a handful of other Israel companies that attempted to mark shemitta in similar ways. These modest, initial experiments suggested that while firms will not unilaterally take voluntary steps to honor shemitta that they perceive as compromising their competitiveness, measures that express corporate social responsibility or that periodically rejuvenate employees and renew company culture every seven years, could benefit everyone.

4. SHEMITTA AND DEBT

> *A year of peace and quiet, where there are no tyrants or taskmasters; "he shall not oppress his fellow or kinsman, for the remission proclaimed is of the Lord" (Deut. 15:2).*

The shemitta-inspired initiatives that gained most traction in the Israeli public sphere were those dealing with debt relief.[12] Chronic household debt is endemic in Israel, blighting lives and shackling families to the deadweight of historic loans that compound until they can never be repaid. While the agricultural roots of shemitta are increasingly distant from a high-tech-based economy, the tragedy of permanent indebtedness is perennial. In 2014, Knesset member Ruth Calderon in consultation with the government's then Chief Economic Adviser, Professor Eugene Kandel, proposed a plan for the government to forgive billions of dollars' worth of debt owed by the country's poorest citizens.[13] However, although the government-funded debt relief never materialized, *Pa'amonim*, an NGO partner of the project which helps families manage

12. Rav Shagar, in a penetrating analysis of the classical sources, argues that the remission of debts is meant to be implemented also in situations falling short of the ideal, complete sovereignty in which the Jubilee might be renewed, but rather which meet conditions of partial, imperfect sovereignty, such as pertain in Israel today. See Shagar, *Gemara Shiurim: Shemitta*, 55.
13. A similar bill was submitted to the Knesset in April 2015 by then Justice Minister Ayelet Shaked, which would have erased 10 billion shekels (about $2.6 billion)

their budgets, crowdfunded money to relieve the debts of program participants anyway. Even after Calderon left the Knesset, some utilities, banks, and other financial institutions proceeded with smaller debt-relief initiatives as a result of earlier conversations with Calderon and Kandel.

A notable feature of these plans was that they engaged seriously with both Jewish sources and with economic theory. The Torah was aware that the promise of a septennial debt moratorium could encourage profligate borrowing that would, in turn, deter lenders from advancing support. "Beware lest you harbor the base thought, 'The seventh year, the year of remission, is approaching,' so that you are mean to your needy kinsman and give him nothing. He will cry out to the Lord against you, and you will incur guilt,"[14] warns the passage on debt forgiveness. The materialization of this very fear led Hillel the Elder to institute the *prozbul* method of avoiding shemitta debt remission, so that loans to the poor would not dry up.[15] In economics, this is known as the problem of moral hazard, which occurs in a contractual relationship where one party is incentivized to take risks at the other's expense, knowing that he will not be required to bear the consequences.[16]

The debt relief plans attempted in the 2014–15 shemitta year were, according to Kandel,[17] explicitly structured, to balance the compassionate goal of debt forgiveness with the concern that the Torah and talmudic

---

in debt owed by about 35,000 Israelis. It was passed unanimously by the Knesset Constitution, Law and Justice Committee, but was never approved on the floor of Knesset, owing to the government calling elections, and so did not become law.

14. Deut. 15:9.
15. Gittin 36a; Maimonides, *Mishneh Torah, Hilkhot Shemitta VeYovel* 9:16.
16. Moral hazard became a well-known expression after it emerged as a leading cause of the 2007–9 economic crash. For example, a mortgage broker working for an originating lender may have been incentivized by large commissions, to originate as many loans as possible regardless of the financial means of the borrower. Since the loans were intended to be sold to investors, shifting the risk away from the lending institution, the mortgage broker and originating lender gained from the increased risk while the burden of the risk fell on the investors. The seminal modern economics article on moral hazard was Kenneth Arrow's "Uncertainty and the Welfare Economics of Medical Care," *American Economic Review*, 53 (5) (1963): 941–73.
17. Professor Kandel explicated these competing considerations in a lecture at the January 6, 2014 Knesset Committee meeting that I attended.

sources raise, that regular debt forgiveness may encourage borrowers to take loans they could never repay. The programs integrated forgiveness of a part of the debt, and rescheduled repayment of another part, together with courses in household budgeting. This combination aimed to give families a new start, while helping them avoid the debt trap in the future. The fusion of idealistic shemitta values with realistic economic thinking seems a promising model for making such initiatives sustainable.[18]

The 2021–22 shemitta year approaches as the Corona pandemic subsides, leaving behind it a trail of wrecked businesses, ruined livelihoods, desperate poverty, and deep indebtedness. In this devastated aftermath, debt forgiveness will likely once again figure prominently in the shemitta-inspired initiatives now emerging in Israel.

5. SHEMITTA AND THE STOCKMARKET

> *There is always a tension between the ideal of listening to the voice inside us that calls us to be kind, truthful, and merciful, and the conflict, compulsion, and pressure to be unyielding that surround buying, selling, and acquiring things.*

Economic life is cyclical. This is true on a macro level and is increasingly the case for individuals. The era of working in the same job, company, or career for forty years is long gone. Rapid technological change leading to the rise, fall, and obsolescence of whole industries causes many to shift jobs and reinvent their careers every few years. Aharon Ariel Lavi fascinatingly suggests that shemitta can be a useful model to help manage this instability.[19] Lavi argues that such changes could be preplanned to mitigate the trauma and dislocation that so often comes with them. Suppose, he posits, that pensions were restructured so that instead of being cashed in at retirement age they could be drawn upon periodi-

18. Debt relief also figured in Diaspora adaptations of shemitta, albeit in a less systematic way. At a Hazon retreat in March 2014, a guest speaker at the event, the comedian Roseanne Barr, secured a $5,000 donation from one retreat participant to relieve the debts of three other participants. Barr also matched the $5,000.
19. Lavi develops these ideas in an ELI video entitled, "Shemitta, Workplan for a 21st Century Economy," and in a forthcoming book.

cally, say every seven years (as in an Israeli *keren hishtalmut*). This could help people to pause, take stock, and reskill in a deliberate way for the next stage in their careers.

National and global economies are also periodic – they go through upswings of growth, investment, and expansion, followed by episodes of contraction and depression.[20] Yet economic theory and policy struggle to understand and effectively address the business cycle. The stock market amplifies the cycle. As business picks up, people invest, share prices rise, people get excited and invest more, still more investors pile into the market, as everyone seems to be making loads of money so effortlessly; there's exuberance and euphoria until a few figure that assets are inflated beyond their real values; euphoria gives way to doubt to anxiety to full-blown panic; people run for the hills, the cycle screeches into reverse, fortunes are lost and the whole thing starts all over again.

The length of these cycles is reliably between six and nine years.[21]

We know that this is true, at least in theory. But in practice, we often forget. This time, everyone says, will be different. There is always some well-grounded economic reason why the current boom will go on forever. But, there is invariably a reckoning. And the deeper the illusions, the worse the reckoning. Moreover, the amplitude between the peaks and troughs is growing, meaning that the destructive power of the crashes is also growing. The 2007–8 crash, triggered by the bursting of a U.S. housing price bubble and the explosion of sub-prime mortgage lending, caused the most catastrophic world recession in seventy-five years. Life savings and pensions were decimated, homes were lost while homelessness, poverty, and misery grew.

---

20. The following thoughts are based on a blog post I wrote: "Shemitta and the Stock Market," *Times of Israel*, November 5, 2014.
21. It is an interesting fact that the final day of two of the last three shemitta years saw two of the three largest falls in the history (measured in points not in percent) of the U.S. stock market. On 29 Elul, 5768, September 29, 2008, the Dow Jones Index fell 777.68 points, a little under 7 percent, the largest daily points drop ever, and on 29 Elul 5761, September 17, 2001, the index plummeted 685 points, the third largest one-day fall in history, a little over 7 percent. Both dates were the eve of Rosh HaShana on the final day of a shemitta year. The "pattern" was not repeated in the 2014–15 shemitta.

In the wake of the 2007–9 crash, leading economists such as Nobel Prize winners George Akerlof and Robert Shiller, picking up on long-neglected insights of J. M. Keynes,[22] used the emerging field of Behavioral Economics to explain how quirks of human psychology can help explain the persistence of economic cycles, and much else. Exploring the sub-rational side to economic behavior that gives rise to such cycles, Shiller writes:

> Irrational exuberance is the psychological basis of a speculative bubble. I define a speculative bubble as a situation in which news of price increases spurs investor enthusiasm, which spreads by psychological contagion from person to person, in the process amplifying stories that might justify the price increases and bringing in a larger and larger class of investors, who, despite doubts about the real value of an investment, are drawn to it partly through envy of others' successes and partly through a gambler's excitement.[23]

We have seen how the command to keep shemitta, "Six years shall you sow your land and gather in your yield, but in the seventh year you shall let it rest and lie fallow" (Ex. 23), is immediately followed by the idea of Shabbat: Six days you shall do your work, but on the seventh day you shall cease from labor. The implication is that just as there is a rhythm to the work week whereby activity needs to be punctuated by periods of rest, so too, a parallel rhythm pertains over a seven-year cycle; we need periods of rest and renewal.

---

22. E.g., "Enterprise only pretends to itself to be mainly actuated by the statements in its own prospectus, however candid and sincere. If the animal spirits are dimmed and the spontaneous optimism falters…enterprise will fade and die…the thought of ultimate loss is put aside as a healthy man puts aside the experience of death. This means, unfortunately that both slumps and depressions will be exaggerated in degree" (J. M. Keynes, *General Theory of Employment, Interest and Money* [London, 1936], ch. 12).
23. Robert Shiller, *Irrational Exuberance*, 3rd ed. (Princeton, NJ: Princeton University Press, 2015), 2.

Seneca excoriated Shabbat as a wicked waste of time. Two thousand years later, the idea that people need a weekly rhythm of work and rest has been embraced by most people on the planet. The message of shemitta – that a similar cycle applies over seven years – has, so far, not.

Yet the charts suggest that such a rhythm is obstinately embedded in human economic life. It seems that we are built to strive and struggle, to invest and innovate, to conceive and create for periods of around six years. During that time, we are apt to get energized, excited, and sometimes completely carried away. The seventh year is meant to be a reset, a return to the real values that underpin our increasingly frantic efforts. If the reset is not expected (and it usually isn't), experience shows that it comes upon us anyway, as a nasty surprise.

What if we could engender the expectation that the seventh year will be a year of readjustment in national economies? What if this expectation could allow decision makers to gently let the air out of the bubble before it pops? Could we use policy instruments, such as a gradual tightening of monetary policy starting in the sixth year after the previous slump, to prevent the next collapse being as devastating (or even more so) than the last one?

These are initial and speculative ideas, offered in the hope that smarter economic minds may develop them in ways that help make our economies more sustainable and resilient.

6. SHEMITTA POST-COVID

> *Stilling the social order from time to time in certain predictable ways is meant to move this nation, when it is well ordered, to rise toward an encounter with the heights of its other, inner moral and spiritual life.*

"But of course, you can't shut down an economy for a year." Such was the unanswerable riposte to utopian speculations about applying shemitta in the modern world. Except now we know that, to a large extent, you can. The unprecedented global lockdown has been something like an enforced shemitta, a compulsory pause in the frenetic busyness of our lives, not just for Israel or the Jewish people, but for the world. All at once, our perpetual motion societies simply stopped. As the Nigerian novelist

Ben Okri wrote in a thoughtful reflection, "It's as if nature is compelling us to be still.... Our whole culture teaches us to run away from ourselves, to run outward into the world, to parties, meetings, work, travel."[24] In making us stop, Okri observed, "it is as if nature[25] were enforcing Pascal's maxim that the cause of all human unhappiness is the inability to sit still in our rooms."[26]

Not that being compelled to sit still in our rooms has been the cause of universal happiness. The pandemic has been, for many, a time of fear and anguish. If Rav Kook spoke of "stilling the social order in certain predictable ways from time-to-time, so we could rise toward an encounter with our inner, spiritual lives," the stillness engendered by Covid has often filled up with worries about children, parents, friends, sickness, suffering, death, bereavement, loneliness, isolation, poverty, jobs, failure of businesses, disrupted education, broken dreams, when will it all end and what will life be like afterwards.

Yet for all that, it has been hard to escape a sharper encounter with ourselves, moments of unusual peace, and some reckoning with the lives we are living.

The pandemic has also enabled us to sense, feel, hear, and smell the interconnectedness of the different spheres of shemitta. A year of Sabbath for workers is also a Sabbath for the earth that they work on as well as a time to support the needy. Before this year, Rav Kook's words about a dovetailing of people and land in the shemitta year sounded like a pretty metaphor.[27] But during Covid, we have seen our inner lives reflected in the natural world. We have experienced the palpable connections between renouncing our routines of driving and flying, and cleaner air, clearer birdsong, and bluer skies.

---

24. Ben Okri, "How We Live Now: Death Hovers Over Us All," *New Statesman*, July 22, 2020.
25. And, one might add, human governments.
26. "All of humanity's problems stem from man's inability to sit quietly in a room alone" (Blaise Pascal, *Pensées*, Paris, 1670).
27. To Rav Kook's contemporary readers, however, they may have evoked the Labor Zionist pioneer A. D. Gordon's concept of *hitpashtut*, the merging of human consciousness with the land, effected by agricultural labor. A thorough comparison of Rav Kook's thinking with Gordon's would be of much interest.

And, when economies are shut down, people who are deprived of their livelihoods suffer and need help. The Torah treats the cessation of work in shemitta and helping the poor during that year in separate *parshiyot,* but we have seen how one self-evidently could not happen without the other. Shemitta insists that we share. We have experienced the choice to respond to the crisis with selfishness or openhandedness; to panic-buy food, hoard hand sanitizer and toilet paper, and look out only for our own, or to reach out to help those who are suffering – whether in the daily heroism of healthcare workers or, for most of us, in calls to the lonely, shopping trips for the elderly, and other small acts of caring. We have seen how freezing whole sectors of commerce causes a huge jump in indebtedness. Indeed, some of the practical measures in process for the coming shemitta year in Israel aim to relieve debts for those whose livelihoods have been ruined.

The comparison of shemitta to Covid should not be taken to romanticize the pandemic. Rather, it de-romanticizes aspects of shemitta. We understand better that observing this mitzva was hard, as the Torah well understood. (Shemitta is the only mitzva about which the Torah explicitly acknowledges the difficulty of observing it.)[28] Indeed, one might well ask, now that we know what happens when we shut down large parts of modern economies for months, why would we ever want to do that again? Of course, we wouldn't – not in the way we have over the past year. Yet we have learned that we *can* change aspects of our lives that were dysfunctional and harmful, but which seemed unavoidable. The enforced pause has helped us break some bad habits. Unable to fly thousands of miles to meetings, people now realize that Zoom works almost as well, and is orders of magnitude cheaper. Companies and employees have tasted the work-life benefits of online working. The optimal post-Covid balance between remote work and in-person offices remains to be found, but it is safe to say that it will involve a better

28. Twice the Torah articulates the thoughts of those who would find shemitta observance difficult: "And should you ask, 'What are we to eat in the seventh year, if we may neither sow nor gather in our crops?'" (Lev. 25:20); "Beware lest you harbor the base thought, 'The seventh year, the year of remission, is approaching,' so that you are mean to your needy kinsman and give him nothing" (Deut. 15:9).

work-life balance and less commuting, pollution, and stress than were normal before. And having seen how the pausing of society brought a rejuvenation of nature, critical environmental problems such as climate change, that had seemed intractable, now appear less so.

A key difference between shemitta and the pandemic lies in Rav Kook's caveat, "… in certain predictable ways." Stopping our societies in unplanned, unprecedented, and unpredictable ways has caused chaos and suffering. As we move from the pandemic into shemitta, one may hope that out of the enforced stillness will emerge smaller, shemitta-inspired, planned, predictable ways of periodically stilling the tumult of our lives and restoring balance to our relationships with nature, our neighbors, and ourselves.

7. CONCLUSION

> *The glory that will appear when shemitta and yovel are observed on the holy land still seems far away; nonetheless our spirits are lifted by what we can fulfill of the mitzvot that are connected to the land, even though what we have is only partial.*

At around the time of the shemitta controversy, in 1910, Rav Kook published an essay entitled *Resisei Or*, "Dewdrops of Light,"[29] which illuminates his larger conception of *Shabbat HaAretz*. In *Resisei Or*, Rav Kook argued that the mitzvot of today are a pathway to a higher ethics of the future that will eventually reach beyond the Jewish people to all living things. Rav Kook notes that Maimonides identified the rationale for many of the commandments with the Torah's struggle against idolatry which took place in the distant past. While praising Maimonides' ground-breaking, systematic attempt to articulate reasons for the commandments, Rav Kook asserts that "in truth, however, the basic principle inherent in the reasons for the commandments points to the future." Our

29. The essay appeared in the *Tachkemoni* journal in 1910. It was published in English as "Fragments of Light: A View as to the Reasons for the Commandments," in *Classics in Western Spirituality, Abraham Isaac Kook*, trans. Ben Zion Bokser (Mahwah, NJ: Paulist Press, 1978), 303–23.

thinking about the explanations for mitzvot should "open up with vitality to the present, and then reach out with gathering strength and light toward a higher future, abounding in idealistic anticipation for a higher life." The mitzvot, in his view, are signposts, or windows through which shines orienting light from the future. The direction of travel "extends to the expanding spirit of humanity." "National consciousness emerges before humanity consciousness,"[30] writes Rav Kook. Mitzvot that today serve the ethical and spiritual cultivation of Israel will come to bear a universal significance and embrace not just all of humankind but also the natural world.[31]

This essay throws light on themes of *Shabbat HaAretz,* which was written at the same time. "The glory that will appear when shemitta and *yovel* are observed on the holy land still seems far away; nonetheless our spirits are lifted by what we can fulfill of the mitzvot that are connected to the land, even though what we have is only partial," Rav Kook writes in the introduction. The social-spiritual vision of this future glory is a frame through which to understand the reasons for current observance of shemitta. As we saw in the introduction to this volume, Rav Kook viewed the current, rabbinically ordained observance of shemitta as a way to preserve the national memory of shemitta until such a time when it could be observed in its fullness. The prospect of what shemitta may one day become enhances the meaning of its observance today.

Moreover, the claims in *Resisei Or* that particular mitzvot will come to bear universal ethical significance – and that intimations of such future significance may inform the meaning of the mitzvot in the present – illuminate moments in *Shabbat HaAretz* that speak to a universal significance for shemitta and *yovel,* encompassing not only humanity but also the natural world. "The particular and the universal are profoundly independent in the most vital and spiritual sense," Rav Kook insists at the opening to his Introduction. With the culmination of seven shemitta cycles in the Jubilee, he declares that "such life-affirming flights

30. Ibid, 314.
31. *Resisei Or* concludes with Rav Kook's well-known argument that in the future we will evolve ethically to embrace vegetarianism and that the laws of *kashrut* are designed to refine and prepare us for this development. Ibid., 317–21.

of possibility (in the Jubilee year) will raise up the people to bind its life together with all humanity." Rav Kook envisages that the realization of the Jubilee's dream of full emancipation will bear a message of hope to all and inspire the Jewish people to understand the universal import of the Torah's teachings: "Then there will arise in the people an inner urge to rein in the separatist element with itself so as to properly highlight the brilliant illumination of the universal."[32]

When, though, is this future whose light might guide our current conception of the reasons for mitzvot? Is it messianic time, or is it a historical era recognizably continuous with our own? Or is this a kind of Maimonidean messianism in which the messianic era will emerge through naturalistic, historical processes, without miraculous intervention?[33] At the end of his biography, Yehudah Mirsky puts his finger on this central question in Rav Kook's thought. Rav Kook believed that he was living in pre-messianic times and that the return to Israel that he witnessed in his day was the beginning of the redemption. Noting that Rav Kook's followers have tended to flatten his complex, dialectic thinking, Mirsky suggests that not all the blame for this can be justly laid at the students' door; this messianic strain in Rav Kook's thought does provide a constant temptation to oversimplification through collapsing the delicate tension between the imperfect now and the dreamed-of future: "Thus, one of the key questions about Rav Kook's place in future Jewish thought is whether the structure of his ideas is entirely dependent on messianic energy to hold all its contradictions together, and just how long that apotheosis can be deferred."[34]

32. Rav Kook, *Introduction to Shabbat HaAretz*, see above, p. 65.

33. Maimonides sets out his naturalistic messianism in *Hilkhot Melakhim UMilḥemoteihem* 11:3 and 12:2, *Hilkhot Teshuva* 9:1, and his commentary to the Mishna of *Perek Ḥelek*. Most recent among the many scholars who have analyzed his views on messianism are Menachem Kellner and David Gillis, in *Maimonides the Universalist: The Ethical Horizons of the Mishneh Torah* (Liverpool: Littman Library, 2020), 282–90. For a classic discussion of the range of approaches to Jewish messianism, from the miraculous to the naturalistic, see Gershom Scholem, *The Messianic Idea in Judaism* (New York, 1971), 1–37.

34. Yehudah Mirsky, *Rav Kook: Mystic in a Time of Revolution* (New Haven, CT: Yale University Press, 2014), 237–38.

Shemitta is an especially interesting test case for Mirsky's question. For as we saw in the introduction, throughout Jewish history, shemitta itself has rested on that fault line between the utopian and the real, around which much of Rav Kook's thinking turns. Rav Kook, like Maimonides and others before him,[35] suggested that while some facets of shemitta may be fulfilled in history, full realization of the soaring ideals of shemitta and the Jubilee will be part of the messianic era.

At the dawn of the 2021–22 sabbatical year, the problems that shemitta addresses – over-exploitation of the earth, overwork, chronic indebtedness, and widespread economic vulnerability – are more acute than ever. Can Rav Kook's thinking in *Shabbat HaAretz* continue to inspire practical steps toward a richer realization of shemitta that falls short of a messianic culmination, yet brings it tangibly closer to fulfillment? Would he have recognized the universal developments surveyed above as stirrings toward that goal? Can we hold on to and cherish the partial ways in which we can observe shemitta in the present while opening to intimations of what it may one day become?

35. Maimonides, *Hilkhot Melakhim UMilḥemoteihem* 11:1.

About Hazon

Hazon, Hebrew for "vision," was founded in 2000.

Today we're the largest faith-based environmental organization in North America. We're leading a transformative movement deeply weaving sustainability into the fabric of Jewish life, and aiming to build a healthier, more sustainable, and more equitable world for all.

We effect change through ***immersive programs***, capable of providing a deeply transformative experience; through ***thought-leadership*** – ideas that help change the world; and through ***capacity-building***, working to support other organizations, projects, and leaders whose vision we share.

We've been working steadily on *shemitta* since 2007, and you can find more information about our shemitta resources and those of our partners at *shmitaproject.org*. Addressing shemitta in thoughtful ways engenders a deeper understanding of the nature of Jewish tradition; and it can and should inspire each of us to bring the values of shemitta to fruition in the world we live in today.

Our work is based at Pearlstone (in Reisterstown, MD) and Isabella Freedman (Falls Village, CT), and we have a wide range of programs and resources for people of all ages and backgrounds. For more information, go to *hazon.org*

Nigel S. Savage
President & CEO
hazon.org | 212.908.2503
25 Broadway | Suite 1700 | New York, NY 10004

Watch "Faith is Green: Jewish Life and Planet Earth," Hazon's TV show in collaboration with EarthxTV – now available free on demand!

As the Jewish lab for sustainability, Hazon is building a movement that strengthens Jewish life and contributes to a more environmentally sustainable world for all.

Maggid Books
The best of contemporary Jewish thought from
Koren Publishers Jerusalem Ltd.